DON'T SUCK

DON'T SUCK

LIFE LESSONS FOR SUCCESS

ANDRE LeCLAIR

ALBERTINE
PUBLISHING COMPANY

DON'T SUCK

Life Lessons for Success

| ISBN | 978-1-5445-3302-5 | *Paperback* |
| | 978-1-5445-3303-2 | *Ebook* |

I dedicate this book to my funny,
sweet mama, Nancy.

CONTENTS

INTRODUCTION

DON'T DO IT

"I'm writing a book. I've got the page numbers done."

—STEVEN WRIGHT

After years in the music business and then real estate, I finally reached a point where I could afford to spend time on a project and not think about the money. So I wrote this book.

Several years ago, I was in a real estate class, and the instructor had just finished writing a book. She shared her experience and was very encouraging. I had an idea for a motivational book based on my life's experiences. It was to be a series of essays, each beginning with a celebrity quote, ending with a life lesson, and presented with a bit of humor.

I had no idea how to write a book, but I knew I wanted to. I googled "how to write a book."

"If you wish to be a writer, write."

—EPICTETUS

I decided to jump in. I had been writing notes and snippets on sticky pads and in journals for quite a while, and it was time to compile them into a book.

Just as I had begun writing the book, I had dinner with an acquaintance. She was a highly successful attorney, and I found her to be remarkably interesting. She had a lot to share about the law, and I was impressed with all of her accomplishments.

I shared some real estate stories, and she seemed interested and amused. As the conversation rolled along, I mentioned that I was writing a book. I had told a few people, to gauge a reaction, and it was always the same. If they knew me well, I got the equivalent of the patting of a child's head, basically because I had never done anything like it before. But many were very encouraging and asked that I let them know when the book was finished.

The attorney's reaction was not quite so positive: "Why on earth would you waste your time trying to write a book? You are uneducated and have no business authoring a book. You really need to spend your time doing real estate and ignore your childish impulses to write a book."

Wow. I was crestfallen. I began to question the book idea and felt that maybe she was correct. Driving home after dinner, I took what she said to heart and decided to abandon the book.

For the next year, I felt like I'd abandoned a dog on the side of a highway. The desire to write the book became stronger and stronger, and I slowly filled my office with sticky notes and notebooks, eventually getting back to the book. My best buddy, Tom, was very encouraging and got me back into it.

I was thrilled to be writing again. Even though I don't have a college degree and can't point to Wyoming on a map, I have stories to tell.

I had allowed one person's opinion and agenda to stall me for a year. I certainly do not blame her. I blame myself for listening to her over me and my gut. Had I not listened, I would've finished much sooner, but this is my book. Live and learn!

LIFE LESSON ──────────────────────────────

Don't listen to other people—listen to your own guidance.

────────────────────────────── DON'T SUCK

(1)

DON'T
SUCK

...AT LIFE IN GENERAL

FERRIS WHEEL

"I see nothing in space as promising as the view from a Ferris wheel."
—E. B. WHITE

Some of my most wonderful childhood memories are from the times my parents took us to the carnival. We loved all the not-so-healthful foods, rip-off games, and unsafe rides. It was kid heaven!

We preferred the carnival at night because of all the lights and action. Nighttime tends to bring out the crazy in people, so the bright lights and nutty carnival goers made it an amazing experience.

The centerpiece of the traveling carnival was the Ferris wheel. It rose above the midway, looking spectacular at night. Round and round it went, stopping every once in a while to scoop up some new passengers or drop off folks exhilarated from the experience.

If you think about it, a Ferris wheel is a lot like life. It's always moving and changing. It can give you a thrill or a stomachache. It has a different vibe at night, and it may break down at any moment. You jump on when it stops at ground level, then make your ascent to the top...and once you reach the top, you begin your descent back to the bottom. You are always at a different place on the wheel.

I believe everything is temporary. No one is on top or at the bottom forever. The top and bottom spots are blips compared to the ascent and descent. This may be disconcerting to realize, but the Ferris wheel of life keeps going round and round—it's ever changing.

We are all on the Ferris wheel of life...on the way up...on the way down...at the bottom...or at the top. So how do you stay on top longer or keep from stagnating at the bottom for too long?

Just know the wheel is always moving, and use that knowledge to your advantage. When you are at the bottom of the wheel of life, focus, work hard, and get that wheel moving. Head to the top as fast as you can!

Now you are almost at the top. This is a place to make important decisions. Smart, enlightened, and successful people know this is a time to put on the brakes. You can never stop the wheel, but by being grateful, thoughtful, and strategic, you can slow the wheel to a crawl and enjoy your success at the top of your game.

And when you careen back down, just relax and don't white-knuckle it. After all, the fall to the bottom is the only way to resume the ascent to the top once again.

LIFE LESSON

Enjoy the ride, even if it calls for a little Dramamine!

DON'T SUCK

GOOD LUCK

"The amount of good luck coming your way depends on your willingness to act."

—BARBARA SHER

Like many other nonprofits, the American Heart Association has interesting and different ways to raise money. In 2004, at a county fair in New Hampshire, the organization was hosting a raffle. I always liked this charity and was thrilled to see that the prize was a spankin' new Harley-Davidson Fat Boy motorcycle. This was unbelievable to me! My friends thought it was a riot, envisioning me on a motorcycle, but I was undaunted.

I plunked down three hundred dollars for thirty ten-dollar tickets. The sweet lady running the raffle told me I would have to fill out my name and address on each ticket. Unfortunately, the boys and I had carnival food to eat and stuffed animals to score, so I quickly scribbled my phone number onto one ticket and hoped she would take care of the rest. "I never win anything anyway," I told the lady. She gave me a wink, and I hit the midway with my buddies.

Fast-forward to two weeks later, and I receive a call at my office. "Hi, this is the American Heart Association calling for Andre LeClair."

I am convinced one of my snarky buddies is playing yet another gag on me. "OK, Jeff, so you are calling from the supposed Heart Association? I think I will plunge my hand through your rib cage and rip your heart out and then pair it with a nice Chianti. When

I am done, I will steal your car and your girlfriend and marry her in Vegas."

"Mr. LeClair, there seems to be some confusion. This is the American Heart Association."

I figure it's time to double down. "Well, Jeff, the local Hells Angels have been told that you think they should wear pink vests and learn some show tunes. They'll be over later to discuss."

"Mr. LeClair, please call 1-800-XXX-XXXX."

I am thinking I owe Jeff an apology as I dial the number. "This month's raffle winner of a 2004 Harley-Davidson Fat Boy is Andre LeClair."

This is unbelievable, and with some therapy, Jeff will recover. I've won a motorcycle!

My enthusiastic dad and I drove to Connecticut to get the bike. "Here it is, Mr. LeClair, a brand-new teal-and-white Harley."

"Chicks love teal," my dad said. I wasn't so sure.

I ended up riding the lovely bike for two seasons. Since I rode in dress pants and leather shoes, I wasn't recruited by any biker gangs. I decided against the giant American flag and stuffed animals. And so it went, the sales guy riding a teal-and-white bike.

The boys had a field day with all of this, but I'd had enough and decided to sell. I listed the Harley on eBay, and a guy from Kentucky bought it for full price. A week later, his employee met me to complete the deal. "Mr. Smith will be very happy with the condition of this bike. He has been searching forever for a teal-and-white bike... for his wife."

LIFE LESSON ───────

Take a chance (and ladies love teal).

GREEN GRASS

"Never envy a man his lady. Behind it all lays a living hell."

—CHARLES BUKOWSKI

"The grass is always greener on the other side of the fence, but it's just as hard to cut." This was one of my grandmother's best expressions.

It seems many people fall into the trap of trying to keep up with the Joneses. As you grow as a person and prosper, you realize "the best things in life aren't things," to quote nineteenth-century writer John Ruskin.

And for those who dabble in the envy space, heed this wise advice from the Buddha: "Do not overrate what you have received, nor envy others. He who envies others does not obtain peace of mind."

Everyone experiences problems, issues, pain, sorrow, and so on. You might have millions in the bank and then, one day, malaria. You get so disoriented that you fall on your face, and three teeth fly out of your head. No amount of money in your checkbook can prevent life's curveballs.

I have always said, "If you want what I have, you have to be willing to do what I do." For many, many years, I worked nearly every day, including weekends and holidays. I wasn't envious of my friends watching bikini volleyball at the beach (maybe a little). I had goals and wanted to achieve a certain level of financial independence.

I traded days at the beach for days of work. I wasn't envious because I was doing what I wanted to do. My friends obviously didn't envy me either—although later in life, a wee bit.

It seems envy is often misplaced frustration over a current situation. If you are unhappy with your life, envy will not make it any better. On the contrary, envy makes things much worse. It's impossible to be envious and happy at the same time.

Life is a series of trade-offs. Take responsibility, decide how you want to live, and happily live that way. Some guys marry extraordinarily beautiful women who might be high-maintenance and snore so loud they scare the dog. No need for envy. Some guys are great athletes, but later in life, they become alcoholics and walk with a limp. No need for envy.

Things usually aren't as they appear, so unless you know the backstory, get off the envy train. Just google someone you envy. You will be shocked. I have endured bankruptcy, divorce, foreclosure, failed businesses, melanoma, knee surgery, a stroke, and COVID-19, and my left foot is dramatically smaller than my right. I became financially secure early in life, so some folks were envious of me.

Instead of being envious, be happy for people. Celebrate their triumphs and successes. Tell them you are proud of them. Send them a note. Give them a call. Buy them flowers!

Know that you can always improve the parts of your life that make you unhappy. Work toward self-improvement, and embrace your current life situation. Enjoy the process.

Your neighbor appears to have perfect hair, a perfect wife, perfect kids, and really green grass? When his wife finds out about his mistress, the grass will be bloody from the ax wound in his head.

Get it?

LIFE LESSON

Envy is not your friend.

FEAR

"Have no fear of perfection—you'll never reach it."

—SALVADOR DALI

Fear is one of the most dangerous of all basic human emotions.

From the time we are infants, we are equipped with the survival instincts necessary to respond with fear when we sense danger or feel unsafe. This is extremely helpful when we are children, but as we enter the real world, it is time to fight fear.

Obviously, fear does have its place even in adulthood:

- You are walking down the street, and five gang members really want your pocket change.
- Your wife is studying to be a barber and needs someone to practice on.
- A pit bull has chewed through his three-inch chain and is running over to say hi.
- Your friend is setting you up on a date with a woman who has a "great personality."
- You are chosen to volunteer at a hypnosis show.
- You actually forgot Valentine's Day was February 14.

Fear has its place in obvious contexts, but when it stops you from doing or saying what you really want to do, that is a problem.

Think about a normal day, and as you recount it, you will see where fear controlled you:

- You don't ask the mechanic a question because you might look stupid. Fear.
- You don't ask the girl on a date. Fear.
- You don't ask for a raise. Fear.
- You don't buy the house. Fear.
- You don't raise your hand. Fear.
- You don't ask for directions (typically men only). Fear.

Analyze your past, and you will see the devastating results fear has caused. Usually, it is fear of the unknown that looms, but in any event, fear will stop you in your tracks and paralyze you. Fear needs to be kept in check—you need to control your fear and not the other way around. Once you take charge, your life will be so much better in so many ways.

I wrote a fear prayer, which I say aloud every morning. I pray to the Universe, but you can pray to God or Buddha or your neighbor Frank. This prayer has helped my life in so many ways:

Fear Prayer

I ask the Universe because I believe in the Universe and my connection to it.

Give me the strength, courage, tenacity, diligence, discipline, and determination to...

Uncover, find, acknowledge, and discover my fears, and then

Systematically and categorically

Eliminate my fears,

For fear is the ultimate determinant to

Personal and professional

Success and Happiness.

Do it anyway because perfection does not exist.

FAIL, FAIL, FAIL

"I can accept failure, everyone fails at something. But I can't accept not trying."

—MICHAEL JORDAN

It certainly seems counterintuitive to embrace failure, but failure is wonderful if you understand its benefits. If you look back at your life, you can acknowledge that you have failed at many, many things.

Babies repeatedly fail at walking, but they persevere and walk like champs in no time. Babies fail at talking, but eventually, they learn enough words to be annoying and make nonstop verbal requests.

Walking and talking become second nature throughout childhood—and right up to the day you do nine shots of Jack Daniels and suddenly fail at both! This common rite of passage can happen in your teens or as late as college, but it's a failure festival! You can never stomach the smell of Jack Daniel's again. So you switch to vodka, and you are fine until rehab.

PERFECTIONISTS

A perfectionist is a competitive person but much more annoying. Perfection doesn't exist, so it's really interesting that people refer to themselves this way. "Perfection is the enemy of the good" is a common phrase, but the original quote from Voltaire is this:

"The best is the enemy of the good."

Confucius makes a great point as well:

"Better a diamond with a flaw than a pebble without."

French impressionist Claude Monet once said, "My life has been nothing but a failure." Remember that the more you fail, the more you learn—and the more you learn, the more you will succeed. Get cracking, and get to failing. You will be glad you did!

LIFE LESSON

Embrace the struggle.

DON'T SUCK

2

DON'T SUCK

...AT GENUINE GRATITUDE

LIFE SUCKS,
THEN YOU DIE

"Nothing is a matter of life and death except life and death."
—ANGELA CARTER

What? This expression is one of the absolute worst. If you believe life sucks, *you* suck! And not to be unkind, but you will probably live too long and make the rest of us miserable.

Life is what you make it. As an old friend used to say, "Life is between your ears."

Life is exactly as good as you decide it will be. We all have issues and problems, but if you are happy, you influence others to be happy. Don't let the Debbie Downers bring you down. Instead, strive to bring the Debbie Downers *up*.

Think of life as a series of ladders. Each person has a ladder and needs to climb to the top. Some people climb quickly, and some people climb slowly, but the point is to climb, at any pace. Unfortunately, some people want to pull other people off their ladders. This isn't pleasant for anyone. Climb up your own ladder and high-five someone along the way.

Just be happy. And if you are not feeling happy, fake it till you make it.

If every day were sunny, we would all burn to death. Plenty of situations will make you upset, sad, or angry, so just be happy when you can. We thank you in advance.

Smile!

BANANAS

"I hate bananas. I just hate them. But I also think a banana suit is the funniest fruit costume a person can wear."

—PAUL NEILAN

Banana is the potassium stick. The fruit is not only good for you, it is also used to describe one's mental condition. "That guy has gone bananas" is right up there with "He's lost his marbles," somehow making mental decay sound like fun.

Bananas make appearances in songs, in banana splits, and on tanning lotion bottles. Confident men in the 1970s wore banana hammocks. Gold-digging men marry older women and then leave banana peels all over the house.

You can drive someone bananas, and every 7-Eleven always has them. Mama's favorite is to refer to someone as a "banana head." You can make a daiquiri with them, and when they are overripe, you can bake up a nice loaf of banana bread. Every single grocery store in the United States keeps a giant carousel of the bright yellow fruit, but bananas are not even grown here.

Where does Walmart get its bananas? Bananas come from Mexico or Central America. They travel a total of 1,717 miles (about twice the distance from Florida to New York City), kept at a temperature of 53 degrees Fahrenheit. Walmart has more than 4,700 stores in the United States alone, and every single store has bunches and bunches, which is frankly bananas!

How unbelievable is your life if bananas are not only plentiful but readily available? For the record, I don't even like bananas, but they are just another reason to be happy and grateful.

LIFE LESSON

Be thankful, and get some potassium.

SPLISH SPLASH

"Television is like the invention of indoor plumbing. It didn't change people's habits. It just kept them inside the house."

—ALFRED HITCHCOCK

Every single day in homes across this great planet, the common morning routine is to head to the bathroom and brush your teeth. This seemingly normal and unexciting activity is the same for most people. You stand in front of the mirror, looking ten years older than you did when you went to bed. Your hair looks like the garage floor broom, and the Sandman went overboard with the eye crud last night.

But you have indoor plumbing, so help is on the way. It's time to brush your teeth. Although this is a commonplace activity, it completely amazes me. I can't believe that by simply turning a handle, clean drinking water flows into the sink. And as if that weren't enough, if you turn the other handle, hot water flows. This is unbelievable.

And your house has a series of pipes connecting the kitchen, bathroom, laundry, and other rooms to running water. The pipes are pressurized. The pressurization enables the water to be available everywhere, even upstairs. Indoor plumbing is amazing—water for drinking, bathing, doing laundry, washing the car, cleaning the dishes, and brushing your teeth!

Years ago, before all this luxury existed, people had to wait for a maid to bring a fancy pitcher of water from the moat and use a stick to brush their teeth. There was no shower or bath—just a funky-smelling person bringing some water to another funky-smelling person. *Yuck.*

The point of all this silly plumbing talk is that people tend to feel entitled to and ungrateful for commonplace things. However, a sense of entitlement is humbled to a position of gratitude once a plumbing issue arises. Life is going along as usual, and then one day, a water main breaks.

You envision a narrow wooden shed in the backyard with a crescent moon cutout on the door. No bathing, flushing, or even car washing—this is not acceptable. *Where is the plumber?*

Eventually, Jeff of Jeff's Plumbing shows up and—*voila!*—hot water for everyone. It was a tough week, and now you are truly grateful. *Now* you are grateful. Jeff, the plumber, drives away, and you are relieved you won't have to see the inside of that disgusting outhouse you'd envisioned.

Jeff's Plumbing, Inc.

We're #1 in the #2 business

Take time to be grateful for all of the ridiculously luxurious amenities we have. Be in awe:

- Running water
- Forty-seven varieties of mustard at Piggly Wiggly
- Cell phones with navigation
- Uber
- Grocery delivery
- Yoga pants (the glory and horror)

Start each day by being grateful for all that is good and all that you have. You will be a much happier person.

LIFE LESSON ————————————————————————————

Be grateful and shower often.

———————————————————————— DON'T SUCK

(3)

DON'T
SUCK

...AT STYLE TRENDS

NEVER WEAR SWEATPANTS

"Nobody ever drowned in his own sweat."

—ANN LANDERS

As we became a more casual society (read: lazy), clothing was designed with comfort in mind. Gone are the days of itchy wool suits or pencil skirts because we want to be comfortable, damn it! As sweatpants gained in popularity, they meant different things to different people.

GYM RAT

Through time immemorial, fitness buffs longed to be comfortable. They came to realize it's really difficult to do jumping jacks in a tuxedo. But I digress...

The gym rats have always worn sweat suits, and thus the name. They work out, sweat, and stink, all in luxurious comfort. Mission accomplished. Sweat clothes are just that—sweat clothes. Workout clothes were never meant to be regular clothes.

PAULY WALNUTS

As with any clothing trend, some folks adapt to an evolved version of the original rendition. Behold the designer tracksuit. If you watch TV's crime series *The Sopranos*, you can marvel at this adaptation of sweats—comfortable yet "classy."

What could be a more wonderful look than Mr. Walnuts strutting around in a royal-blue tracksuit, complete with bright-white loafers? Add a gold chain or two, and you have a feared tough guy. The look was, um, elegant yet casual. You liked it...*or else!*

THE COMFORT CREW

The trend started when folks decided to just wear sweatpants or pajama bottoms in everyday life. In my humble opinion, this is disgusting. It makes us look like a lazy, unkempt society.

But here is the problem: folks who wear pajama bottoms or sweatpants in public do so because they probably haven't showered. They got out of bed, pulled on their sweats, and headed out to Denny's for pancakes and eggs. They may even do some yard work and then go to Chili's for a few beers and a plate of nachos. But one thing you can be sure of is there was not a bath after yard work and before Chili's. And there certainly wasn't a shower between bed and Denny's.

To reinforce this trend, think of wearing a baseball cap because you are having a bad hair day or have severe "bed head." I know, I know...this could really ruin your people-watching, but it's an uncomfortable fact of life.

The big question is this: who decided this is OK? Be a good human, shower, and put on a pair of pants before you go to Waffle House. Society will be impressed and thankful.

People who DON'T SUCK only wear sweatpants to the gym or to a *Sopranos* convention.

LIFE LESSON

Wear pants when you go out for pecan waffles (they are worth the extra money).

DON'T SUCK

BATHING SUIT

"I go to Vegas now, and I'm in the casino, and I'm gambling, and there's a guy in a wet bathing suit gambling right next to me."

—SEBASTIAN MANISCALCO

In the 1970s, I was very fortunate to live in a wonderful home in northern Massachusetts, complete with an in-ground swimming pool. Our family's fearless leader was my dad, who was fun and funny and loved to do skits, gags, and tricks to make everyone laugh.

Dad was the party guy with the proverbial lampshade on his head. He had a never-ending supply of ideas, constantly producing new and inventive ways to split our sides.

One picture-perfect summer day, we invited several relatives and friends to our house for a pool party. My grandmother, a couple of aunts, and their friends were thrilled to hang out at the pool. It was hot out, and the booze was flowing.

Dad was noticeably missing. He had gone into the house but was there for quite a while. Aunt Milly thought I should check on him. I was just going to finish my Coca-Cola and head that way when the door opened.

With a loud "Hello, everyone," Dad appeared in a woman's oversize hat, my mom's sunglasses, and a multicolor bathing suit. As he sashayed across the lawn toward the pool, the old ladies howled. What did he have up his sleeve this time?

He made his way through the group of ladies, stopping to touch and kiss them and compliment them on their beauty. It was like a drag show. He then walked the length of the pool to the deep end and stepped onto the diving board.

With a dramatic hand gesture, he removed the hat and sunglasses, tossing them to the side. Now that he had everyone's attention, it was time to do some muscle poses. He was five foot eleven and weighed 170 pounds. A competitive bodybuilder, he was not. After a couple of spins and then a dramatic step, step, and a jump down, he propelled himself up, and he was airborne. The dive was a perfect ten and so entertaining!

The crowd watched Dad glide underwater until he popped up in the shallow end to an enthusiastic round of applause. He waved to the crowd, slipped back into the water, thrashed around, and emerged with his bathing suit dangling at the end of his extended arm.

The ladies were hysterical as he waded toward the ladder to get out of the pool. The first rung of the ladder...now the ladies covered their mouths. The second rung...they tried to look away but really didn't want to.

Up and out of the pool...smiling widely to a chorus of cheers and jeers, Dad was sporting the bathing suit he had on under the other one.

LIFE LESSON

Be authentic, have fun, and buy extra bathing suits.

TATTOOS

"Tattoos aren't fun unless you're an idiot. It's not fun to get tattoos."

—RIFF RAFF

If tattoos are really important to you, go for it. I personally do not understand tattoos.

Honestly, they bother me more when I see them on a woman than on a man. I feel that a woman's body is a work of art, and adding tattoos is like spray-painting graffiti on a statue. Would you buy a Porsche and spray-paint your name on it?

NO LAUGHING MATTER

At a comedy show a few years ago, one comic started his set by asking for a show of hands from audience members who had tattoos. A lot of people raised their hands. Many were women.

He then said he dates *only* women who have tattoos. As the tattooed lovelies swooned, he explained, "I only date tattooed women because they knowingly and enthusiastically do something they will absolutely regret later!"

In my humble opinion, if you want to cite poetry, convey that you like butterflies, or showcase the image of a loved one, a tattoo is a weird way to do this. I suppose if getting extra attention is important to you, it makes sense. But when I see Chinese letters on someone's neck, my best guess is "beef and broccoli?"

It seems tattoos are a must for bikers and carnival workers. And lots of young women seem to like how they look all tattooed up. This will be an interesting look when they are senior citizens.

BUSINESS OPPORTUNITY

Tattoo-removal services are becoming more and more popular. When Courtney breaks up with Dave, the tattoo of his face on her thigh will be hard to explain to Jim.

Tattoo regret could make for a very lucrative business!

Maybe this will change, and my words will become outdated. But for now, try to control yourself and the urge to tattoo your entire body. You might later regret it.

By the way, if I ever decide to ink up, I will go all out and get a Mike Tyson face tattoo.

LIFE LESSON ——————————————————————

Ink is for pens, but if you disagree, always spell-check before tattooing.

——————————————————— DON'T SUCK

4

DON'T
SUCK

...AT CAREER ASPIRATIONS

SCHOOL

"A child educated only at school is an uneducated child."

—GEORGE SANTAYANA

This is a tale of five Joes:

Hourly Joe is a former carnival worker, skipped 83 percent of high school, smokes a lot of weed, plays cards and video games, and lives in a third-floor walk-up apartment. He has girlfriends with multicolored hair, piercings, and tattoos. He drinks whatever beer is on sale at Piggly Wiggly, where he gets an employee discount. High school degree? Almost. He lands a job in a factory, screwing caps on toothpaste tubes. He dates one heavy girl and one skinny girl, who hate each other. He smokes a lot, loves mac and cheese and Little Debbie snack cakes, drives a car that's missing a hubcap, and has tattoos and an infection from a nose ring. Being broke is a badge of honor. $

Trade School Joe is not handsome, plays pool and darts, lives in the loft of a barn his dad built, works on a '72 Chevelle in his front yard, has girlfriends he can't lift, drinks Red Bull by day and Bud at night, and eats only McDonald's drive-thru or Domino's carryout. He has an Apprentice Plumber license and gets a job with a plumbing company. He buys a mobile home and a Harley, adopts his wife's three kids who call him Big Papa, buys an expensive pickup truck with a back seat, fishes but rarely catches anything, and has an overgrown lawn due to an eternally broken lawn mower. He's always dirty and tired, and he never smells good. $$$

Average Joe College is handsome, plays football and baseball, lives in a two-bedroom condo, has girlfriends with short, blond hair, drinks beer, and is in great shape. He has a college degree in business management, lands a sales-related job in a big company, and learns to play golf. He marries at twenty-five, has two kids, and lives in a house with a nice lawn. $$$$

Exceptional Joe College is kind of handsome, plays chess or difficult video games, lives with his parents, has girlfriends who wear running shoes with summer dresses, drinks beer and eats Doritos, and is a bit pudgy. His master's degree in engineering gets him a job that pays very well, but he's not taken seriously for promotions because he wears a baseball hat to work. For after-work entertainment, he sets up a video-gaming room in his apartment, where he lives with his sister. He doesn't have a lawn. $$$$$$

Entrepreneur Joe is average-looking, reads personal and business development books, invests in the stock market, paints houses, and has a landscaping business. He buys a single-family home, even though he has no family. He has a no-nonsense, pretty, ambitious girlfriend. He doesn't smoke, drinks two vodkas with soda per night, and devours meat and potatoes. With his Master Plumber License, he takes over his dad's plumbing business, builds it into a multimillion-dollar company, and continues to live with the girlfriend he won't marry. He travels only to places that are hosting business seminar conventions, has an impressive stock portfolio, and never does plumbing. He smells good, always! $$$$$$$$$$$$$$$$$$$$$

As you can see, you can do well with a traditional college degree and very well with a specialty college degree. You can also do very, very well as an entrepreneur, and best of all, you can start at the bottom and end up at the top.

In America, you can succeed with almost nothing going for you, but you will find an easier path to great success if you constantly read, attend seminars, and learn everything you can about your business and about life.

A successful software engineer is typically very well educated. A successful entrepreneur is also very well educated but perhaps from the "school of hard knocks" or self-education. Either way, there is simply no way around it. To be successful, learn, learn, learn.

LIFE LESSON

Everyone goes to school one way or another.

DON'T SUCK

ATTACHMENT

"I have made this letter longer than usual, only because I have not had the time to make it shorter."

—BLAISE PASCAL

When I was twenty-two, I played bass in a club band. I ran a tight ship, and an agent suggested I get into the business side of music. This seemed like a perfect side job to gigging six nights a week. The club routine was getting old, and although the benefits were outstanding, the money was lousy.

I decided to venture back into the wedding band business via gigging and booking. I landed a job at an entertainment agency that booked a slew of clubs and hotels. I would head the wedding band division. This was comical since I had no experience or formal education and had never actually "worked."

Sitting at my desk, which was the size of Rhode Island, I had to do my typical "fake it till you make it." I knew the wedding band business but was not exactly skilled at shuffling paperwork and drafting contracts. Luckily, the company had a secretary (before they became admins) who happened to be the boss's wife. She was lovely, attentive, and incredibly adept at keeping a business running smoothly.

It was time for Agent Andre to send a sales letter to Julie, the bride.

Dear Julie,

How's it going? Getting married must be cool. I mean, I can't imagine, but if you think it's a good idea to commit to Jeff for eternity, who am I to judge? Well, if you are convinced that a wedding is a better investment than a duplex in Somerville, I am happy to help you book a band. We have some wicked good bands that will have your guests partying their asses off. I stapled some band info sheets to this letter. If you and Jeff want to check them out some night, give me a holla.

Later, Andre

With all the confidence of a know-it-all young punk, I handed the scribbled sheet of paper to Carol. I will never forget how gracious she was while I stood and watched her read it. I was right there if she had a question only a salesman could answer. "I'll type it up and bring it to your office when it's done," she said.

I had some pencils to sharpen while she drafted my customer follow-up letter. All at once, she was in my doorway, smiling and handing me the letterhead and envelope.

Dear Julie,

Congratulations on your engagement! Thank you for choosing Musicorp to assist you in finding the perfect band for your wedding. Our band roster features the absolute best entertainment choices for your special day. Attached, please find information on a few of our top bands.

We look forward to working with you.

Regards,
Andre LeClair
Entertainment Consultant

This was such an eye-opening learning experience for me. Any company benefits from professionalism in every phase of their business. I had always been able to sell, but because I lacked formal education, I didn't realize the importance of letter writing, contracts, and other types of written communication.

To this day, I use "attached, please find" and "regards" and have become much savvier at business. Thank you, Carol Fini. May you rest in peace...

LIFE LESSON

Music is a business.

DON'T SUCK

READY, FIRE, AIM

"If you have a dream, you can spend a lifetime studying, planning, and getting ready for it. What you should be doing is getting started."

—DREW HOUSTON

I have been involved in several businesses and ventures in my life. I made most of my life and business decisions despite discouragement from many friends, business associates, and family members.

I ascribe to the business philosophies of "ready, fire, aim" and "follow your gut," which go against much traditional thinking. It's notable that the loudest voices against new ventures or ideas often come from the very people who are scared, set in their ways, and not very successful.

- I was told to get a college degree.
- I was told to get a job with a big company.
- I was told not to buy individual stocks.
- I was told musicians cannot make a living.
- I was told to get up early every day.
- I was told not to buy Florida real estate in 2010.
- I was told not to buy medical office space.
- I was told karaoke was a stupid idea.
- I was told not to open a no-alcohol nightclub.

- I was told not to drive old vehicles.

- I was told not to dress for court.

- I was even told not to author a book!

This is just a partial list of things that I have done against the well-meaning advice of others. Granted, some ventures were more successful than others, but I was always successful when I listened to my gut. I followed my instincts and decided to follow the advice of only the people in my life who went against conventional wisdom.

Millions of people are unhappy, unfulfilled, and unsuccessful. They would just love for you to join them. Do not ever join them.

If your heart and gut are yelling at you, listen. You will not be sorry.

LIFE LESSON ————————————————————————

Listening to your gut is never wrong.

———————————————————————— DON'T SUCK

DON'T COMPETE

"If you think you can do better, then do better. Don't compete with anyone, just yourself."

—BOB FOSSE

"There is no competition." A business partner of mine has always preached this expression. His point is that if you are great at what you do and work like hell, you will rise to the top, and there won't be anybody else up there.

It's been proven that if you spend all your time trying to compete with others, you miss opportunities to make yourself and your business greater. Unless you are a professional athlete or into beauty contests, being competitive is a fool's game.

HORSE RACING AND OPRAH WINFREY

In an interview, Oprah Winfrey explained that closely monitoring the talk-show competition distracted her production team from what they needed to do to produce a number one show. She told her team they had to be like racehorses with blinders on either side of their eyes so they could look ahead at their own lane only.

As consumers, we tend to react to certain forms of competition. The big-box stores have competitive price-matching programs that seem alluring until you see the fine print. You must jump through a million hoops, and in the end, you only matched a price—what a waste of time.

CAR DEALERS

You are in a car dealership, and the salespeople are competing against one another for a fifty-dollar Cracker Barrel gift certificate. All the while, they are hoping you will not notice the car is lime green and does not have power windows.

For the sake of this stupid competition, you try to buy a car from a twenty-seven-year-old kid whose right eyebrow is higher than the left. He is wearing a suit that is way too tight, and his cheap cologne can't cover up his three-pack-a-day habit.

REALTORS

For some reason, realtors always tell you how many millions of dollars in houses they've sold and how the number is way above most other realtors...*blah blah blah*.

Some great realtors take Oprah's racehorse approach, but that leaves the rest of the field to the irritating competitive bunch. They have their big board in the office to highlight the top and humiliate the bottom. Real estate is truly the business of the braggadocious.

Competitive behavior makes people look conceited, unapproachable, and unlikeable. "Big hat, no cattle" is prevalent in these circles. Work hard, work on yourself, stay in your lane, and play nice.

LIFE LESSON

Cracker Barrel is overrated, so compete only with yourself.

XTENSION

"I invented the cordless extension cord."

—STEVEN WRIGHT

For thirty years of my life, I made a living in the wedding music business. I ran the business from a home office and kept the music equipment in a two-car attached garage. It was a bit intrusive to my living space but well worth it to have to work only a few hours a week.

The neighbors always wondered why I rarely worked and why I got the mail at the end of the driveway in my pajamas. It was very Tony Soprano! "Is he infirmed, mentally ill, a drug dealer, the lazy brother of the guy who owns the house?"

I cared not one iota. I was young and made a great living working Saturday nights and a few hours during the week. The intense (easy as fishing) schedule afforded me time to work on my business. I was always trying to better the band, which I lovingly referred to as a "product." We were always learning new tunes, buying better equipment, and thinking of new ways to market the product.

"There is no competition" is a concept I came to understand deeply. Observing my competition, I found that many made glaring mistakes and, as a result, could not command the strong money that came with better gigs.

It seemed many of my colleagues thought like musicians and not like businesspeople. Personally, I think the purview of "I am an artist, so I can't relate to real-world issues" is a lot of nonsense. I never understood the allure of being a starving anything, let alone a musician. I was more interested in fortune than fame. Plus, I looked better in a suit than a tie-dyed shirt and sandals.

Because fellow musicians and bandleaders were enthralled with promoting their unique brand of annoying original music, few bothered to have presentable sound systems and gear. Broken-down speakers, unsightly amp racks, scratched speaker stands? Unacceptable and unprofessional.

For some reason, bands had an affinity for plastic milk crates. These sturdy, stackable crates were perfect for mic wires, extension cords, and other accessories. Stamped with *Hillshire Creamery*, these dark-green crates didn't seem out of place in dive lounges and clubs. I always felt bad for the dairy farmers. They ordered and purchased these crates to deliver milk, only for many of them to be stolen and used by aspiring rock stars.

This was all perfectly wonderful until a band got booked for weddings. Just imagine the wedding director, Travis Whitmore III, watching the band load crate after stolen crate into his five-star hotel ballroom. I found this to be a fantastic opportunity to increase market share, and I went to work.

I brought our equipment to a company that manufactured road cases. I wanted the drums, speakers, amps, and all the gear to be fitted for custom tour cases. This was an expensive exercise but well worth it. We said goodbye to the milk crates and hoped a new generation of musicians would adopt this long-standing tradition.

We also ditched all the orange extension cords—the kind used to trim hedges—and replaced them with custom black extension cables that could be easily hidden onstage.

We bought a box truck with a lift gate, and we were ready to be a professional wedding band.

Hotels and event centers appreciated our hip and classy setup and referred us like crazy.

Since my retirement from the wedding band business, I've made good use of the orange extensions. I can now trim my hedges that are way on the other side of my property!

LIFE LESSON

It's all in the presentation—milk crates are for milk.

DON'T SUCK

5

DON'T
SUCK

...AT MUSIC APPRECIATION

TONY BENNETT

"I think one of the reasons I'm popular again is because I'm wearing a tie. You have to be different."

—TONY BENNETT

Show-and-tell? Are you kidding me? I was working at a very young age on saving for retirement, and now I had to concern myself with show-and-tell? Kindergarten had arrived. As I was deciding what craft or talent I would present to my fellow classmates, I realized this could actually be fun.

Wait, I had a great idea! It was important to my dad to expose me to the music he loved, ultimately a wonderful thing we shared for years to come. My dad was a huge fan of Tony Bennett, and on Sundays, he and I listened to his records. I could do a song for these little brats!

I took out my Easter suit and wore it to school that day. As an aside, it's important to point out that my beautiful, hardworking parents loved and encouraged me. They knew they'd created a kid who was a bit different, but they let me be me. OK, back to show-and-tell...

I always walked to school, and that day, I had a bit of a Rat Pack swerve. Life at age five was pretty cool! I walked into class dressed to the nines, and I settled in for the show.

First up was Craig. Craig had brought his stamp collection for the class to enjoy—a snore fest for even the most studious. OK, Craig probably forgot about show-and-tell and was scrambling that morning. I can picture his father wearing a sweater vest, chain-smoking, and delighted to offer his stamp collection. Evidently, the Civil War was a treasure trove for Mr. Hadley and his collection. This dusty, musty, uninteresting notebook was not exactly what five-year-old kids dream of. It was a notebook with lousy-looking stamps that weren't glued in place. The stamps unsticking and floating to the floor were the best part of this show.

Next up was Kim. Kim had made a dollhouse out of Popsicle sticks. The house had no windows or doors, and it smelled like cherries. Unfortunately, Kim had thirteen cavities from eating the ninety-seven Popsicles that she culled for their sticks. Kim seemed too young to be five.

Then it was Joe's turn. Joe had painted eyes, a nose, and a mouth on an odd-sized rock and called it his pet. Joe was taller than everyone else in class, and since this was his third try at kindergarten, we expected more.

And now Andre was about to sing a song that not one kid would know. "Boys and girls, Andre LeClair will sing 'Who Can I Turn To' by Tony Bennett." I sauntered up to the front of the classroom and belted out my heartfelt rendition. As the teachers poked each other and the kids shrugged, I was sure I'd nailed it. A cameo performance at the faculty holiday party seemed within reach.

Popsicle Kim cried. My teacher sent me home. I think she was in shock, as she was clearly in over her head. It was a long walk back home.

At dinner, my dad asked about my day. I told him that normal kids didn't understand Tony Bennett. I went on to tell him about Kim and asked if I could borrow the car in thirteen years.

Be authentic, and use your voice.

START

"Start where you are. Use what you have. Do what you can."

—ARTHUR ASHE

At twelve years old, I picked up a guitar on a whim, and by removing the top two strings, I had a bass guitar. It did not have to be a perfectly tuned bass. I started with what I had. I didn't wait until I had the money to buy a nice, shiny instrument. I grabbed that guitar with the missing strings and played bass for hours. I knew I had a long way to go before I had a shot at becoming a member of Earth, Wind & Fire, so I just worked with what I had.

I had a unique talent in that I could hear bass motion. Once I heard a tune, I could play the bass line in any key. I believe it's called "bass ears," which doesn't sound very flattering.

I got a radio, dialed it to a Top 40 station, and simply started playing bass—no lessons, no idea what I was doing. I just started. That day was the start of my career as a bass player and my foray into the music business.

I never became a world-class player because I was more interested in the business of music, but I held my own. I played in bands for years and years. I played by ear and never learned how to read music. Playing bass proved to be a million-dollar decision!

I eventually bought an actual bass. It was decent and sounded good, but it wasn't expensive or fancy. That was never important to me.

Years later, when I was part of a busy wedding band, we held auditions for a new drummer. Drummer after drummer showed up for the audition, most with elaborate drum setups—shiny, beautiful drums and lots of gleaming cymbals. The drums were so much more impressive than the talent level of the drummers who auditioned. The money they'd spent on drums would've been better spent on music lessons. My bandmates and I were getting discouraged.

Suddenly, a broken-down car pulled up with a tall, scruffy guy who had a bunch of broken-down drums. The crappy drums were not even in cases. The guy was dressed in a Hawaiian shirt and shorts, and he set up the junkiest drums ever. When he asked for duct tape to secure the hi-hat to the floor, we got really nervous.

Much to our surprise and delight, this drummer was one of the most musical, in-the-pocket drummers I had ever heard. He was a naturally gifted musician. It was such a stroke of luck, and we were over the moon!

As we chatted after the audition, he told us he had fallen on some tough times and was starting over. Rather than waiting to save enough money to buy new drums, he started with what he had and from where he was, to boldly move forward.

I had the pleasure of gigging for years with this talented drummer. He eventually formed a successful wedding and event business in Albany, New York. He still plays, but now his drums are worth more than my car. Mike is a killer drummer, successful businessman, and close personal friend. Actually, he is one of my idols.

LIFE LESSON

Just take off from the starting line.

JOHN THE FARMER

"A gentleman is a man who can play accordion but doesn't."

—UNKNOWN

"Ladies and gentlemen, what time is it? *It's polka time!*"

Long ago and far away in a small New Hampshire town—next to its dot on the map, it says "actual size"—was a smoke-filled Chinese restaurant lounge. It was at the height of the karaoke craze, and a farmer named John was broadening the horizons of a bunch of mai tai guzzling singers. *America's got talent? You bet! Right here at the Star Wars bar!*

It was the early 1990s, and karaoke was king. The so-called singers sang to cheering, enthusiastic regulars who hoped for cheering and enthusiasm when it was their turn to sing. Liquid courage kept the singer list full, and Advil kept the servers from quitting. It was magical.

John was a big ol' farmer who stood about six foot four in overalls and a sport coat, and he was the happiest guy in the world. Friendly and confident, he had a smile that could stop traffic. He walked up to strangers to chat, and people just loved him.

One fateful night, he decided to sing. I wasn't sure about this. I had zero experience with chicken-raising, karaoke-singing farmers. Could bar patrons endure another rendition of "Friends in Low Places" or "Folsom Prison Blues"? Maybe I was overthinking it, but we were all about to find out.

The booze was flowing, the smoke was burning everyone's eyes out, and John the Farmer was ready to sing. He downed a few Bud

Lights as he patiently waited his turn. He turned in his song choice slip, and I was even more nervous. It was a rowdy crowd, so this could go either way.

"Ladies and gentlemen, it's time now for...John the Farmer!" He made his way up to the stage. "It's polka time!" The system cranked out the intro to "Beer Barrel Polka," and the crowd went crazy. *Whew.*

John the Farmer grabbed the mic, and in that moment, all was good in the world. Even the drunkest person in the place was a little more intoxicated because, damn it, it was polka time!

The audience clapped and cheered, and John was on fire—three minutes and seventeen seconds of polka bliss. People sang and hugged like World War II had just ended. It was epic!

Even though most people rarely heard polka in their daily lives, you would never have known it. It was magical. John ended the tune to a giant round of applause. He took a bow and made his way out of the stage lights to a sea of fans. Evidently, very drunk women love a polka-singing farmer. A star was born!

"Ladies and gentlemen, next up, Mary will sing 'The Rose.'" And just like that, we were back to the stark reality of lousy singers, huge bar tabs, and tomorrow's dead-end job with a terrible hangover.

John sang his polka every week for a few years, and every week it was a joy. John, wherever you are, thank you!

As country singer-songwriter k.d. lang has quipped, "To dance is human; to polka is divine."

Roll out the barrel and bring joy to people!

BOWL

"Nobody in football should be called a genius. A genius is a guy like Norman Einstein."

—JOE THEISMANN

I was brought up in a family that discouraged sports and encouraged music. My parents were both musicians, and my dad thought sports were a waste of time. We never watched sports, played sports, or cared about sports in any way, shape, or form. For exercise, we were encouraged to engage in physical labor, but as far as playing baseball or football? Forget it.

Dad's philosophy was that if you pursued music, you could make money as an amateur musician. Lots of musicians play in clubs or at weddings, parties, and so on. You don't need a hit song. All you have to do is learn hit songs, and before you know it, you have gigs.

In sports, it is not the same. You can become a pro athlete and make millions, but if not, the alternative is playing on a softball team sponsored by Acme Towing. You start in Little League, and if you are lucky, you are a high school star. If you are fortunate, you get to play in college, but that's usually the end of the road.

Ten years later, you find yourself drunk in a Chinese restaurant, chatting to an uninterested guy about your high school days as captain of the football team. All the while, a bunch of geeks from high school are in the band, playing "Sweet Caroline," getting chicks, and making money.

Later in life, Dad's advice proved to be right for me. I made a great living playing other people's music and never once had to see an orthopedic surgeon for a sports-related injury. I had money in the bank and the use of both knees.

This was wonderful, except I never played or watched a sport. And although the number of working musicians is a small group, the number of people who understand and watch sports is everyone.

In my late twenties, I moved into a nice suburban neighborhood in southern New Hampshire. Everyone had a minivan, 2.3 kids, and a good-looking spouse, and they all played every sport imaginable. My house had a pool table, a velvet poster of dogs playing poker, a swimming pool, and typically a stray musician or two.

It was a quiet place to operate the business during the day and party at night. On weekends, we played weddings, parties, and clubs. The neighbors eventually figured out my late hours were because I was a musician and not a drug dealer. It was a fun time!

One day on my morning run, a neighbor flagged me down to invite me to a Bowl party on Sunday. I was thrilled to accept as I happened to not have a gig. *What do you bring to a Bowl party?* I wondered.

I walked two houses down, and my smiling, sorta drunk neighbor greeted me at the door. I handed him my lovely glass bowl, and I walked in. He seemed a bit perplexed about the bowl, and this seemed odd to me as he was the one who'd insisted on a party theme that made no sense. He didn't seem to even appreciate my bowl. "How's the music biz, Andre, and what's up with the bowl?" He handed it back to me.

We walked into the living room, and it was packed with yelling, drunken men watching football on a big-screen TV. Evidently, there is a special football game called the Super *Bowl*. Who knew?

No one even noticed me, so I walked into the kitchen carrying my lovely bowl. It was like walking into heaven. The kitchen was packed with wives of the Neanderthals who were watching the game. The women were beautiful, smelled good, and cared about football about as much as I did.

"Are you the musician guy that lives down the street?"

"Yes, I am, and I never was much into sports, so that's why I have this bowl."

"Oh my God, you are funny and adorable. Please hang out with us. Vodka tonic?"

"Group hug, ladies?"

It was the greatest sports day of my life. I group-hugged the ladies while the real men were fixated on a game where men in spandex pants tackle one another.

Thanks, Dad. You were right, and I love you for it.

LIFE LESSON

Play ball? Learn to play an instrument instead.

DON'T SUCK

6

DON'T SUCK

SUCK

...AT KICK-ASS CELEBRATIONS

SEVEN-DOLLAR TRICK

"What I like to drink most is wine that belongs to others."

—DIOGENES

My fun-loving parents loved to entertain. Our home was the place where everyone wanted to party. We had lots of space and an in-ground pool, and my parents were wonderful hosts.

I have fond memories of going to the store for beer, ice, and all kinds of food. Weekends were a blast, and all the cool people came to our house. My parents were musicians, so whenever the pool party started to wind down, the party moved to the living room.

We had a grand piano, an upright bass, and drums. Many nights the joint was jumpin' until the wee hours. I noticed that certain guests always brought things—wonderful homemade food, flowers, desserts, wine, or beer.

Other guests came empty-handed. It didn't seem like they were too poor or cheap but instead as if they felt entitled. This was aggravating to me, as my parents worked very hard and always served great food and alcohol that cost them plenty.

People loved our parties, and most brought gifts. The folks who didn't, somehow disappeared from the guest list after a time.

Years later, my dad told me about his system. He didn't care if a guest brought flowers picked from the side of the road or mittens his wife knitted, but to show up empty-handed was a sin in Dad's eyes.

Although we never did get any terrific knitted clothing, we obtained our share of wine—all types and sizes, and usually in the seven-dollar price range. Remembering this was an aha moment for me. The idea was to buy a thirteen-dollar bottle of wine on sale for seven dollars and put it in a wine bag from the dollar store. Now I was a preferred guest for less than nine bucks.

If you are set on spending only seven bucks, you can forgo the wine bag for certain parties. If you are invited to a fancy dinner party, you can still use this method, but do not write on the wine bag tag. Chances are there will be others that do the same, and the hosts will never figure it out.

Finally, make sure you buy wine that has an expensive-looking label. You will never drink it, but it needs to look pricey!

LIFE LESSON

Flowers are nice, but wine is better,
so be a good guest and never feel entitled.

DON'T SUCK

HALLOWEEN

"The worst thing about Halloween is, of course, candy corn. It's unbelievable to me. Candy corn is the only candy in the history of America that's never been advertised. And there's a reason. All of the candy corn that was ever made was made in 1911. And so, since nobody eats that stuff, every year there's a ton of it left over."

—LEWIS BLACK

In New England, Halloween is a favorite holiday. It's the perfect combination of pretending and hustling. Back in the day, Halloween was strictly celebrated every year on October 31, which seemed to always fall on a weeknight. Trick-or-treating began after dark and continued for two to three fun-filled, sugar-high hours.

Fast-forward twenty years, and I was a thirty-something with no kids, living in a quiet, upscale suburban neighborhood. I was in the music business, and mine was the party house. The yard was presentable with the grass always mowed, but inside was like a frat house.

We all gathered after gigs, the parties starting after 1:00 a.m. Used, crappy furniture adorned most rooms except for the billiard room. The kitchen was stocked with Solo cups for beer and paper plates for pizza. The refrigerator was exclusively for beer and date-expired condiments.

As mid-October approached, we were all gainfully employed as it was the height of wedding season. Craft beer and three-topping pizzas were proof we were flush.

The last Saturday night in late October, it was typical that we would gather after 1:00 a.m. to consume adult beverages, debrief, and make fun of the weddings we'd just played. Little did we know that in our enlightened town, Halloween was not necessarily celebrated on October 31.

We partied like rock stars until the wee hours to prepare ourselves for Hangover Sunday. Billiards, booze, and broads—life was so good that even Frank Sinatra would've been proud.

It was noon the following day, and I was peacefully passed out in the doorway between the kitchen and dining room with a beer in my hand and a piece of pepperoni pizza folded neatly in my top pocket. *Ding-dong*.

Had someone forgotten his girlfriend? As I opened the door and the sun hit my unshaven face, I looked down to see...a miniature ghost, a short and stocky princess, and a skinny firefighter. It was time to Google "Betty Ford Center," but first, I had to deal with these little brats. "Trick or treat!"

"Stay right there, kids." What on earth could I give these excited little punks? Stale chips and salsa? A frozen hot dog? Beer? Cigarette butts? Wait, the spare change jar! "Kids, we are out of candy at the moment, but here is some money so you can go and buy some candy cigarettes. Please keep this between us, OK?"

This proved to be a very costly Halloween. The following year, kids arrived by the busloads.

LIFE LESSON

Stay up to speed with the holidays,
and always be resourceful.

GRAVY WALTZ

"Ballroom is two people dancing together to music, touching in perfect harmony."

—ANTON DU BEKE

My dad was an incredibly talented lounge singer. He sang at nightclubs, lounges, and weddings throughout his life. It was his side gig and hobby, but he sang a lot and made money over the years.

When he reached his golden years, Dad got the opportunity to sing in a big band comprised of a bunch of peers he had gigged with over the years. The musicianship was strong, and it was a very tight band. They did quite a few gigs in the Boston area.

As a big band that played ballroom-type music, they were a hit with the older folks fondly referred to as the "Q-tip crowd." The challenge was that the bandleader was a jazz musician and not an entertainer. He was more interested in keeping the musicians happy than entertaining the crowd of dancers.

The cotton heads had a blast "cutting a rug" to the big-band sounds and sang along with Papa as he fronted the band. With a dance floor packed with dancers having a ball, the band leader suddenly called out the tune "Gravy Waltz." This jazzy, snappy tune was cool, but it cleared the dance floor because its tempo was way too fast. Those who managed to dance to it looked like they were dancing on the sun.

The musicians loved it because they got to play extended solos. The dancers hated it because they weren't interested in the musicians impressing themselves. It was not great overall for pleasing the crowd.

My dad always called me Sunny because I was so bright. "Sunny," he said, "always remember that you are hired to entertain the people, not the other musicians." My papa was spot-on. Heeding his advice, I had a very successful career as a bandleader in a Boston-based wedding band for many years.

LIFE LESSON

Get over yourself, and play to the people if that's your job.

DON'T SUCK

DAVE

"I definitely like the oddballs. There's a song called 'Little Thing,' which is the only song that I have recorded that has no words. And it's the one that I get past my critic inside me."

—DAVE MATTHEWS

This is a story about the Dave Matthews Band. Actually, it's a story about a bride who was a huge fan of the Dave Matthews Band—a client named Meahgyn. The bride's silly and fancy spelling of the traditional Megan was no match for her love of the Dave Matthews Band.

This client sought to become a standout bride by doing unusual things. We knew from the start this would be a challenge, but we were prepared to make wedding history...or at least have a story to tell.

Another client had referred her, and after reviewing our band video and song list, she booked us for her wedding. She was excited for a fun event, and we were excited not to have to get day jobs.

A month prior to the big day, Meggy Meg and I had a conference call to discuss music and the flow of the event. We suggested she use our song list to highlight songs she wanted and cross off "do not play" tunes. This was a common approach to customizing set lists for weddings.

Everything was proceeding without a hitch until Miss Mego let us know she adored DMB and wanted us to play *a lot* of his music at the wedding. Our cherished client's wedding reception was at a major Boston hotel with a guest list of more than 350. I knew that unless these 350 guests were from her sorority, DMB would not be the best choice for most of the playlist.

I diplomatically suggested that since she had invited a varied age group of family and friends, she may want to keep the music more mainstream and traditional. I told her we loved DMB and would be thrilled, but since her wedding was a one-shot deal, DMB may not work very well. So we agreed to learn four DMB tunes.

Do not get me wrong—even though I don't particularly care for DMB, I acknowledge that it's a great band. But my vast experience told me we would be heading down Bridal Disaster Street. This bride was insistent that her wedding would most certainly be the wedding of the century if DMB numbers were the focus of the music. The bride had spoken. [Sign of the cross.]

The wedding day arrived. Everything looked wonderful, and the guests looked excited to have fun. For a moment, I forgot about the big, gigantic DMB anchor.

Dinner was lovely, and you could feel the amped-up energy in the room as it was time to get the party started. "Ain't No Mountain High Enough" was our first song, which instantly packed the dance floor. The place was alive, and everyone—young and old—was having a ball.

Oh, wait. As the song says, "Here comes the bride."

"Andre, remember our meeting? DMB is going to bring this party to a whole new level." She sure was right about that! We played the first DMB tune and instantly lost half of the dancers. How could this be?

Song number two left the bride and six of her friends dancing self-consciously while the rest of the guests sat at their tables. Song number three? Only the bride and her maid of honor graced the dance floor. Success! DMB music had successfully alienated 348 guests. This wedding reception now officially sucked.

As the bride finally realized DMB was better in concert than at a wedding reception, she approached the band once again. "Andre, play something else. You guys are ruining the wedding."

Vindication? Andre's inner voice: I'll bet Walmart greeters get a free vest.

We reached down into the freezing wedding ocean and rescued 348 guests with "Sweet Caroline."

LIFE LESSON

Trust the professionals.
And thanks, Neil Diamond.

DON'T SUCK

THOUSAND-DOLLAR DIVE

"This life is like a swimming pool. You dive into the water, but you can't see how deep it is.

—DENNIS RODMAN

Because Dad had a big job and Mom was sick of taking us to the park, we were the first in the neighborhood to have an in-ground pool. As a kid, it was just unbelievable to have such a wonderful amenity. We took full advantage.

Because of New England's weather, the typical pool season was from Memorial Day to Labor Day. It was a bit chilly at the beginning and end of the season, but we were tough New Englanders, weather-worn little brats.

As soon as May hit, my friends and I tore off the days on the calendar until the big pool opening day. Soon our skinny bodies donned Evel Knievel swim trunks to take the first plunge of the season. It was quite a ceremony.

Our heroes—Dad, Uncle Roger, some guy named Marty, and his friend Sputnik—were hard at work getting the pool open. The beer was flowing, and the air was thick with Marlboro smoke. We were hanging with the big boys and learned a few new swear words to boot.

Suddenly, with one big tug, the pool cover was off. Dad gave us the cue, and we jumped into the leaf-laden, freezing water. We flew out as fast as we'd entered, and summer pool season was officially open.

Dad broke out the chemical test kit and began his special chemistry—twenty-six gallons of Clorox bleach and two pounds of baking soda. "Boys, we call this better living through chemicals."

The next day, the water was crystal clear and 68 degrees. With shivering bodies and blue lips, we stayed in until someone offered us something to eat. We dedicated our lives to our vinyl-lined paradise. We swept the deck, cleaned the filter, and vacuumed the pool bottom. It was the most wonderful playground on the face of the earth.

Fast-forward to twenty years later, and I would buy a house with the exact same style pool. The skinny, exuberant kid who loved freezing-cold pool water was now an overweight, cranky real estate investor with little time to enjoy or maintain a pool—the pool opening, the chemicals, the filter, the vacuum cleaner. It was expensive, time-consuming, and just awful.

I usually opened it sometime in June and tried to get the cover back on in August. To get my money's worth, I always did one dive in the middle of the summer. It was my thousand-dollar dive. I hated my pool.

I eventually sold the house and moved to Florida, only to buy the house back seven years later. When I returned, I was all but retired and looked forward to the grand old pool and entertaining all summer. I could afford to maintain it and enjoy it. I had worked hard for a long time, and I now appreciated the pool like I did when I was a kid.

The pool supply store suggested a robot vacuum, which made maintenance a breeze. I was still known as the man who opened and closed his pool as fast as possible...and, of course, for my yearly thousand-dollar dive.

My pool and yard became the place where everyone wanted to hang. I loved my pool!

LIFE LESSON ———————————————————————

Be appreciative of what you have, and be a kid again any chance you get.

———————————————————————— DON'T SUCK

7

DON'T
SUCK

...AT GOOD HOUSEKEEPING

LAWN TRACTOR

"That's the great thing about a tractor. You can't really hear the phone ring."

—JEFF FOXWORTHY

In my late twenties, I bought my first house. I had been living in a condo complex for a few years but felt it was time to join suburbia—wide open spaces, neighbors who have stuff you can borrow, swimming pools, movie stars!

Living in a condo had some great advantages and a slew of disadvantages. Condominium living allows you to discover not only the horrid smell of curry but also the horizontal habits of adjacent neighbors. It also means someone cuts the grass, trims the hedges, and vacuums the common hallways. The chores get done and not by you. You observe the work and wave like you are royalty.

Condominium living also comes with a lot of rules. You cannot park in certain areas nor play the ukulele at 4:00 a.m., and you cannot dry your underwear on the pool fence. You must take the Christmas decorations down before Memorial Day, and naked pool deck aerobics is frowned upon.

Suburbia is a whole different game. You have a yard, and if you are lucky, it's an acre or two. You can play the clarinet 24/7, and you can even pee outside. But the absolute best part is that you can own a lawn tractor. As soon as I'd bought a pool table, my next purchase was a lawn-cutting machine.

Evidently, some men really like lawn tractors. It may have some evolutionary explanation that has to do with wild antelope and grass cutting, but every single one of my neighbors had one.

So, I went on over to Sears. Kevin had been assistant manager for outdoor power equipment for nineteen years. Legend had it that he'd sold nearly a thousand of the coveted grass-cutting go-karts—$995 on my credit card, and it would be delivered in a few days.

To prepare for the first cut, I made sure I had a beer for the cup holder and my Sears baseball hat. All summer long, I drove the tractor. Where else can you drink and drive? I was hammered, and the uneven lines in the lawn proved it. It was a great machine—electric start, and it ran forever on a tank of gas. I named it the "Marquis de Sod."

One day while I was driving under the influence, the tractor stopped dead. How could this be? It was filled with gas and had only been running for about a six-pack. This was awful and needed to be fixed ASAP.

Luckily, I had a friend who had a truck and liked to fix things. *The lawn wasn't going to cut itself,* I chuckled. The next day, my friend arrived, hopped out of his truck, and walked over to Marquis de Sod to see what was wrong with the old boy. He pulled on a stick-like thing that was about four feet long. I was happy to be rid of it if it had made my tractor stop. He muttered the word "dipstick," which I thought was an unkind name to call me.

"You idiot!" he exclaimed. "When did you last check the oil?" I was perplexed, assuming it had been checked at the factory. He explained that the engine was seized. It would cost more to fix than to buy a new tractor. He called me a dummy and drove off with Marquis, half a Bud Light still in the cup holder.

LIFE LESSON ————————————————————————

Learn basic things in life, such as the crucial importance of oil changes.

—————————————————————————— DON'T SUCK

CHEERS

"I may be drunk, Miss, but in the morning, I will be sober, and you will still be ugly."

—WINSTON CHURCHILL

I was buying rental properties by age twenty-five. I was also living large and drinking like a fish.

Scanning the for-sale listings one day, I found a condominium being sold "as is." The photos showed a property full of trash. Evidently, its former occupant had mental issues and was a hoarder. The trash was three feet deep. We could barely open the door, and it was impossible to navigate the trash and check out the place.

What luck! I boldly made a low offer with no inspection. I had a feeling that once the trash was removed, the unit would be a profitable rental. Because I was the only buyer crazy enough to make a cash offer with no contingencies, my offer was accepted.

We filled a forty-yard dumpster. We couldn't believe a human had lived in such a trash heap. But my hunch turned out to be correct. With a good cleaning, new carpet, and a paint job, the unit would rent fast for strong rent. "Fortune favors the bold."

Purchasing the unit was also a breeze, sort of.

I signed the documents and paid the deposit, and thirty days later, it was time to close the deal. Back before we made all real estate purchases via bank wires, people used certified bank checks. On a rainy, gloomy morning, I was more hungover than usual, but I dressed in a suit and tie and headed to the bank.

"Hi, Rose. May I please have a cashier's check in the amount of $35,000? Please use funds from my real estate account." She passed a withdrawal slip through the window along with a pen. I was a bit shaky, and holding a pen was just not going to happen. *Damn hangover*. I told Rose I was having muscle spasms and that I would return later to sign.

If I knew I was going to be this thirsty today, I would've drank more last night, I thought. I was thirsty and needed to stop the tremors. *Wait, the liquor store opens at ten, and it's a short walk down Main Street.*

"May I please have a half pint of Dr. McGillicuddy's Mentholmint Schnapps?" My theory was that although I was drinking booze at 10:00 a.m., it was developed by a doctor, so it seemed the best medical course of action.

Three gulps, forty-five seconds of full body warmth, a twinkle in my eye, and I was ready to sign. I could've signed the Declaration of Independence. I strutted back to the bank, smelling like a drunken street person with minty fresh breath.

A quick scribble, a cashier's check in the amount of $35,000, and I was back in business. Just six hours until Happy Hour!

LIFE LESSON

Don't try to outdrink a fish, but do buy real estate.

IDIOT

"As usual, there is a great woman behind every idiot."

—JOHN LENNON

Our property management business was stressful, rewarding, fun, and aggravating as hell. Our rental portfolio featured units in apartment-style buildings. Each building housed thirty different "families" living in one big building with some nice shrubbery and palm trees out front.

The problem with this arrangement was the building's single water source. One giant pipe serviced all thirty of the units, and the water was then piped to each individual unit. Each could be shut off at the unit but not always.

We quickly found that what was a headache for us was a Hawaiian vacation for the plumbing companies. They weren't afraid to charge for their work, and we were always happy to see them. Property managers and plumbers are the best of friends.

Whether you cause it or are the recipient of it, everyone hates plumbing issues.

"Everyone is an atheist until they clog a toilet in someone else's house."

Tenants are people, and people are sane or crazy. We always said, "Humans are amazing."

In our workflow, we sometimes had to call a plumber to make a repair that necessitated shutting off water to the entire building. If we knew in advance, we emailed the residents, but in an emergency, we couldn't.

Several fun aspects came with this, depending on the time of day. In the early morning, people showed up in our office sporting towels and soap horns. Evidently, when water stops mid-shower, it's quite an issue. Who knew? This didn't happen often, but when it did, it was joyful.

It also happened at non-shower times like midafternoon. This affected stay-at-home moms, college students, and tenants who worked from home. These groups took to their cell phones like drunks to an open bar.

We were always a bit amazed at the phone calls, which usually came from the same people. We lovingly referred to them as "the idiots"—behind their backs for obvious reasons. Some idiots know they are idiots, but some don't.

The complaint calls were all basically the same every time:

"This is unit 304, and we don't have any water."

"Is there a reason we don't have water?"

"We've tried every faucet, and none of them have water in them."

"We have no water, and I need to take a shower right now."

"How are we going to wash our dog?"

The fun part was that we had no idea. The building's water was shut off because a plumbing issue needed to be fixed. A plumbing problem never goes away by itself, by the way. The short answer was that the water would be back on when the issue was resolved, but after a while, we decided to have some fun.

The angriest tenants got the silliest answers:

"Did you pay your water bill?"

"This always happens prior to nuclear war."

"Do you still have TV?"

"Now do you see the value of showering every day?"

"Maintenance should have the outhouses built by next week."

"The whole town ran out of water, so let's hope it rains."

"Hope you aren't serving spaghetti tonight."

As the saying goes, ~~shit~~ stuff happens. Go with the flow—yes, the flow.

LIFE LESSON

Try not to be an idiot.

DON'T SUCK

20 X 40

"Somebody said to me, 'But the Beatles were anti-materialistic.' That's a huge myth. John and I literally used to sit down and say, 'Now, let's write a swimming pool.'"

—PAUL MCCARTNEY

At one point in my life, I was convinced I had it all. I had a really nice house with a beautiful in-ground pool, I was making money, I had money in the bank, and I was at the top of my game. I had a great social life, wonderful friends, and a killer car. Life was good.

One balmy New England summer night, I decided to shut out the world and just hang out by myself at the pool. I really liked to grill, so I had a pile of chicken and was ready to go.

I dove into the deep end of the pool and had a refreshing swim. The water was crystal clear and the perfect temperature. After drying off, I settled into a relaxing night—vodka and soda with lemon and a Davidoff cigar. I was thrilled I had hired a service that sprayed for mosquitoes. Chicken was grillin', and Andre was chillin'.

As I stood by the grill, I noticed the pool's water level was a bit too high. This was an easy fix that involved setting the filter to backwash, which would lower the water level. What a life! If only I had a butler to fetch me another vodka. A few steps into the kitchen, a lemon squeeze, and I was back in business. Hey, I wasn't driving, so I let the vodka flow.

The chicken was grilled to perfection. I headed inside to make a salad and another vodka. Delicious! I was feeling no pain. *Man,*

I sure make wonderful chicken! I'll drink to that! I'll clean everything tomorrow. Where's my cell phone? Some lucky recipient was about to receive my first vodka-induced call of the evening. After gloating to a few buddies, I reconnected with an ex who would be thrilled to hear from me. *How can I be out of lemons?*

Nightcap? You bet! Where is my left shoe? It had been a wonderful night. I stumbled upstairs to my bedroom. I put the TV on to see what those crazy Sopranos were doing and eventually drifted off. *Good night, everyone.*

Six a.m. arrived sooner than expected, and I'd definitely lost the boxing match. As I made my way to the bathroom, I glanced out the window. It was a beautiful, hot summer morning, and the pool water had evaporated. *Wait, what?* Lord, I had never shut off the backwash, and now my pool was a giant hole in the ground.

Me: "Hi, this is Andre LeClair. Someone stole my pool water."

Pool supplier: "Thirty thousand gallons? *Hey, Kevin, it's LeClair. Wait until you hear this one.*"

Me: "Be kind. I think I have a summer flu."

One hour, five tanker trucks, six thousand gallons of water, two seriously amused pool techs, a puke bucket, a lemon, a cigar stub, a few chicken bones, and $1,300 later, my pool was back in business.

Why is my towel ringing?

Thirty thousand of anything is a lot, so pay attention and don't drink alone.

AISLE 7

"Ever consider what pets must think of us? I mean, here we come back from a grocery store with the most amazing haul—chicken, pork, half a cow. They must think we're the greatest hunters on earth!"

—ANNE TYLER

I have never been a fan of food shopping. I tend to stock up all at once, as opposed to shopping regularly. The idea is to get all the stuff and get out. It's all about efficiency. A few trips a year, and I have all I need. But there is a lot of stuff on each trip.

So, there I was, happily cruising down the aisles and whistling Christmas tunes. My dad whistled Christmas tunes year-round. Apples don't fall far from trees.

"Attention, shoppers. Extra-thick pork chops on sale today. Thank you for shopping at Food World."

This was going to be a great day. *I think I need dish soap.* Aisle 6, Ajax brand, and it was a two-for-one special.

"At Food World, double coupons every Wednesday."

With my carriage about two-thirds full, I rounded the corner on aisle 9.

"Attention, shoppers. Please check your cart to make sure you didn't accidentally swap your cart with another shopper."

People are so stupid, I thought. I did a cursory look in my cart— pork chops, Ajax, coffee, Cap'n Crunch. *It's not me.* Whistling "Sleigh Ride" (it was July, by the way), I hit aisle 12.

"Attention, valued Food World shoppers. If you have the wrong cart, please come to the service desk to swap it."

Maybe I was too smart to shop at Food World, and perhaps Piggly Wiggly would be a better choice. Aisle 15, ice cream. *I wonder what the total calories in a gallon—*

"Dear shoppers, Sara is patiently waiting to swap her cart. She is here at the courtesy desk."

I wondered what would happen as some poor, hapless soul shuffled over to Sara, apologizing profusely. Home stretch. Checkout was wide open—what luck. "Can you believe how stupid a shopper has to be to not recognize what's in the cart?"

"Uh, yeah, paper or plastic, sir?"

"Plastic, please." Man, I had a *lot* of stuff—pork chops, Ajax, bottled water, Cap'n Crunch, low-fat coffee ice cream, eyeliner, baby food, tofu, tampons...*Uh-oh.*

"Sir, are you OK?"

Be aware of your surroundings—you may meet Cap'n Crunch!

(8)

DON'T
SUCK

...AT ROMANTIC ENDEAVORS

WEDDING SURPRISE

"People make assumptions when you're not married. I've been best man at five weddings, and I said I'd never do it again 'cos everyone got divorced."

—DAVE CLARK

After years of playing weddings and corporate events, we became better and better at creating weddings that were well run and fun. As we gained experience, we found it necessary to enforce certain policies.

We developed a "no surprises" policy we used for each and every event. Roughly two weeks prior to the big day, I met with the future wedding couple to discuss the flow of the event as well as music selections for the formalities and dancing.

We had the couple complete a form in advance to customize the details, so the meetings were efficient. At the end of the meeting, I told the couple we had a policy that would not allow surprises at the mic, on stage, or through our speaker system. I offered examples:

Two bridesmaids named Meaghan and Megyn telling a story about a Barbie camper and a beheaded Ken doll

Groomsman Seth with a dramatic reading from the Kama Sutra

Auntie Linda delighting the crowd by teaching them how
to knit an ashtray out of asbestos yarn

I then shared another example that happened at one of our weddings. This is a true story...

Way back in the day, we recorded music onto cassettes to play when the band was on break. This was particularly helpful during the band's dinner break. We popped in a cassette of smooth jazz tunes and ate along with the guests. After dinner, we got the party started and played dance music until the end of the event.

It was a Saturday night at a nice country club in Massachusetts. The band was on break and gathered in a side room, eating dinner and having fun just being together. A groomsman found the band and asked if he could have a word in the hallway with the bandleader. I was the bandleader, and my gut told me this might not go well.

This cat was six foot four and looked like a WWE superstar. I sensed that he could easily kill me with his bare hands, but I hoped I could accommodate his request.

"Take this cassette, and go and play it now. It will be really funny—it's a surprise." He was serious, and three of his fingers were tattooed. I don't scare easily, but I also didn't want to upset Brutus. *Wait, our policy!*

I quickly walked to the head table and asked for a word with the groom in private. Thor had gone back to his table, so we went to the hallway to talk. I handed him the cassette tape, which was labeled "First Night." He looked at the tape and pulled me into a bear hug. (This wedding was getting weird.) He was visibly shaken and thrilled I'd saved the wedding.

As it turns out, "First Night" was a recording of the bride and groom during sexy time. He had placed microphones under the bed and was able to capture everything from bed squeaks to God references.

Thor was asked to leave the wedding, and I was a hero.

LIFE LESSON ⎯⎯⎯⎯⎯⎯⎯⎯⎯⎯⎯⎯⎯⎯

Romantic surprises can be fun but not at the expense of someone's dignity.

⎯⎯⎯⎯⎯⎯⎯⎯⎯⎯⎯⎯⎯⎯ DON'T SUCK

BAD DATE

"It is an extra dividend when you like the girl you've fallen in love with."

—CLARK GABLE

I was fifty-three years old, financially stable, and had just moved to Southwest Florida. I decided it was time to dive into the dating pool. Anyone who has ever swam in this pool of hope will tell you that, with few exceptions, it's awful and demoralizing.

Florida is a unique place to live—wonderful beaches, sunny and warm weather year-round, and a retirement haven. If single and in your fifties, you quickly discover the three Bs—booze, boobs, and Botox.

On the surface, this might seem like it could have some potential, but one begins to realize that between the gold-diggers and husband hunters, it's a jungle out there. If you are an attractive woman and have no scruples, eager men will wine and dine you seven days a week.

I fondly referred to this type of dating as "foodie calls." A foodie call is when you feed a person you don't know and will never see again.

I dated as often as I could stand, which was very seldom. I had businesses to run and was trying to preserve some of my dignity. However, I met a woman online.

Her photos were marked as "current," which is code for "taken a decade ago." She fit a profile that was fairly typical—a single mother with a bunch of divorce money. The money was to remain safe and secure in her wallet, only to be used at the mall or for endless manicures and pedicures.

This woman was looking for someone to make her laugh and liked long walks on the beach. She posted twenty-seven photos of Fluffy, so her new man had to like cats. He also had to be honest, unmarried, and could not be living with his mother. I seemed to check all the boxes, except for my allergy to cats, but this was going to be a "foodie call," so the cat would never be an issue. Every single man is allergic to cats, by the way.

Date night arrived. We met at a local hipster restaurant for drinks, which really meant I would be paying for food because she didn't have time to eat all day and was very hungry. We sat at a table in the bar and were greeted by our server, Megan (misspelled *Megyine* on her name tag).

I spend lots of time in restaurants, and I genuinely appreciate bartenders and waitstaff. I hold them in very high regard. If not for them, I would be eating mostly mac and cheese, Hamburger Helper, or Burger King drive-thru. I always engage them, treat them like a friend, shake hands, ask their name, crack jokes, and try to include them in my night out.

My date, Deborah (not Debbie), was tan, nicely dressed, and had that fake dating personality I had come to expect. She also seemed to suffer from an overinflated sense of self-worth and did not share my admiration for the waitstaff. Megan was in for it.

~~Debbie~~ Deborah was demeaning, rude, condescending, and downright nasty. I was embarrassed and insulted, but I had an idea. I excused myself to go to the men's room. I headed for the back of the restaurant and found Megan. I apologized for my crappy date, gave her a handful of cash and a wink, and asked her to guide me to the back door.

Twenty minutes later, Deborah texted, *Are you OK?*

I texted back, *I am home with my friends, Mac and Cheese. You are an awful person. Enjoy your dinner, and be sure to leave a good tip!*

LIFE LESSON

There is always a way out.

MUSICAL CHAIRS

"If it's the right chair, it doesn't take too long to get comfortable in it."

—ROBERT DE NIRO

Nightclub owners often ran promotions on off-nights to drive sales. Weekend nights were always busy, so the idea was to create a weeknight that was so desirable that it felt like a weekend. The cirrhosis crowd jumped at the chance to mix, mingle, and get their drinks on.

"People go where people are" was the battle cry, and a Wednesday night was the perfect spot between sucky Monday and TGI Friday!

It was a time of expansive growth for this New Hampshire town just over the Massachusetts border. *Live Free or Die* was emblazoned on every license plate. (Ironically, the plates were made in state prisons by prisoners who hopefully had a good sense of humor.)

Construction was booming, industries were growing, and it was time to celebrate. The Manor IV was located in the non-entertainment capital of the world—Nashua, New Hampshire. Friday and Saturday nights at the IV were off the charts. The best bet was to take your grandparents to dinner at 3:00 p.m. and then head over to get in line. Everyone was well dressed and thrilled to be there.

Patrons entered to blaring music, super-hot girls who smelled good, and enough booze to ruin everyone's morning. The marketing department had been publicizing Wacky Wednesday every weekend for weeks. *No cover charge! Games and prizes! Nonstop fun!*

The first Wednesday was an enormous success, and the club owned Wednesdays for many years. It was crazy to have to wait in line on a Wednesday, but once you noticed the hottest girls were allowed to cut the line, you did not mind one bit.

The average age of patrons was mid-twenties. Most were not yet married, so they were extra happy and motivated to find someone to ruin the rest of their life—or at least a willing participant who understood the walk of shame.

Wednesday night. The place was hopping, the booze was flowing, and life was good. The energy was as good as a weekend, so tomorrow would bring challenges, but for now...*who cares?*

Suddenly, the music stopped, and a guy in a sequin jacket with perfect eyebrows sauntered onto the dance floor. As he fired up the ~~drunks~~ patrons, members of the staff brought several chairs onto the dance floor. *No way.*

I tried to get to the back of the room while my friend flexed, did jumping jacks, and cracked his knuckles. He was serious, and I was concerned. I counted twenty chairs. Plenty of volunteers were extremely interested in the hundred-dollar prize.

Round and round they went, playing musical chairs. Stop! *Sorry, buddy.* Music on. Round and round. Stop!

A perplexed guy swore he'd said, "Table for two." He will be late for work the next day. And on it went. Fewer chairs, fewer people. Shattered dreams. I hoped my friend Paul would win a hundred dollars. *Oh no.* It was down to four people, and Paul was still in.

Now three people remained: 1) Paul, 2) a big guy who could not catch his breath, and 3) an extremely sweet-looking girl who needed rent money. Round and round. Stop! *Ba-Boom.* The big guy was out.

Paul cracked his knuckles again (I was not sure why), but I thought it might not go very well. Round and round and round. It took forever. Stop! The girl flew through the air, and Paul sat in the chair.

There was a weird silence as Paul jumped onto the chair and threw his hands in the air. The silence turned into booing and people yelling, "You suck!"

Paul scanned the crowd, looking for me. I looked at my feet. Eyebrow boy declared him the winner to more intense booing. This could be the end of Paul.

In a moment of clarity, Paul grabbed the hundred-dollar bill, walked over to the sweet girl, dropped to one knee, and handed it to her like a proposal.

It was unclear if her tears were from injuries or joy, but Paul was a king. *Thundering applause.*

LIFE LESSON

Stay classy.

DON'T
SUCK

...AT SOCIAL GRACES

FIGHT CLUB

"Everyone has a plan until they get punched in the mouth."
—MIKE TYSON

This may sound basic and more geared toward men, but...never get in a fight. Never.

Unless you qualify for the Golden Gloves, are a master at Mixed Martial Arts, or have a black belt in judo, you will surely regret it. Fighting is like karaoke. It's better left to professionals.

Having spent a good deal of my life in bars, as a musician as well as a patron, I know fights are fairly common. The more booze, the better the chance—people are mixing and mingling, and they're drunk.

Fights can be sparked by love triangles. Or maybe some guy is just frustrated and unhappy about his life, secretly wishing he was six foot four. Perhaps he hated being the youngest of three, did prison time, or is mad his soon-to-be ex-wife is getting half the house, and his half is the exterior.

Maybe the crazy guy is *you*, and you are ready to rearrange some guy's face because he accidentally slept with your wife. The excuses for throwing punches in a Chinese restaurant lounge are as varied as the preferred blends of alcohol in a Scorpion Bowl communal cocktail, but the time to fight is never.

If you think it might be fun to break someone's jaw, you could end up in court or have to get a tooth surgically removed from your knuckle. If you happen to miss and then take one to the kisser, you could spend lots of time in dental surgery and end up with teeth you put in a glass before bed.

If it seems a fight is brewing, act fast to diffuse it. This could be a challenge if the guy has booze-infused muscles or is with a crew of guys ready to spring into action.

Let's say you are drinking a few high-octane beverages, excited to meet Cindy at the bar. You met Cindy on Tinder, and although she lied about her age and then claimed Tinder didn't allow her to fix it, you feel a special connection.

Cindy likes honesty and loves to laugh. She is "not a skinny Barbie doll type." She didn't post full-body photos, but she has a lovely dog and a poem tattooed on her left foot. If you are looking for a one-night stand or booty call, "swipe left right now." Cindy is not that way. She is looking for her "split apart," and although you don't know what that is, it sounds like it may be fun.

Is that Cindy? She seems like she needs to be taller. Maybe she won't fit in your car, so odds are she has a great personality. This becomes the least of your worries as she notices her former lover Jeff is in the house. Jeff is bigger than your backyard shed and spends a lot of time at the tattoo parlor.

Jeff takes one look at you and Cin Cin, and he is ready for battle. This can't be the way to get on *The Bachelor*. He mumbles something about taking it outside, which you think is a great idea until you realize he wants you to join him.

Do you smash him in the face with your Polynesian glass? Crack a chair over his head? Do some fake karate moves? Or buy him a drink? Handing your Mastercard to a waitress is the best way to retain your pearly whites. Say something flattering and funny, and get the hell out of there.

Jeff and Cindy seem perfect for each other, and you just saved a bundle not buying her dinner.

LIFE LESSON

Never fight—dentistry is expensive.

DON'T SUCK

IT'S BETTER TO BE KIND THAN TO BE RIGHT

"Too often we underestimate the power of a touch, a smile, a kind word, a listening ear, an honest compliment, or the smallest act of caring, all of which have the potential to turn a life around."

—LEO BUSCAGLIA

Often in life, we are faced with situations and people that are challenging. You can call a blue sky a blue sky, but sometimes people just don't agree, can't understand, or are confused. Do not fret. Just be kind.

Do you choose honesty over kindness? Here's a pop quiz:

- Your lovely wife is confused about her weight and asks you for clarification.
- Your seven-year-old wonders how many times you would like to hear "Old MacDonald" on the clarinet.
- Your friend Jay needs feedback on his karaoke rendition of "Greatest Love of All."

Honesty? Nope. Kindness.

HIGH OR LOW?

Roger knows the market value of his home because he talked to Brandi, who works part-time at 7-Eleven. Brandi not only *almost* passed the Florida real estate exam, but she also has a RE/MAX tattoo on her wrist. Roger has a crush on Brandi, and after his house sells, he plans to marry her and have free coffee for life.

So what do you do if you are Roger's prospective Realtor? Do you tell Roger he is delusional? Hell, no!

You very professionally and delicately tell him you appreciate his wisdom but that, based on your research, Brandi's take on home prices might not be accurate. You then tell him that he and Brandi make a nice couple, praise his Velcro shoes, and buy him a donut. Be kind!

MOSAIC MANSION

Again, let's say you are a Realtor. You take a listing with the understanding that the seller is going to have some fancy and beautiful tiling done. You wait for a month, and the big day arrives. The seller is excited as he beams over pallets of tile he bought on closeout. For this discussion, "closeout" means it's dumpster-ready.

The tile is awful and mismatched, and it's *everywhere*—floors, closet, walls, and yes, even the ceiling. It's loud and cold, and the seller is ecstatic. He is convinced a person with class and fancy taste will pay more than asking price to live in such splendor.

Do you tell the seller his place looks like a prison shower? Nope.

You tell him a person with discerning taste will love the echo effect in the kitchen and that tile is so easy to clean. You then express your gratitude for his business. Be kind!

MENOPAUSE MONDAY

You hire a new admin, Donna, who just turned fifty-eight. She is sweet, can type 120 words per minute, and really understands the real estate business. What's not to love?

Donna settles in and is working away when you notice a sheet of ice has formed on your desk. You check the thermostat, and lo and behold, it's set to 51 degrees. Donna is at her desk, sweating like a long-tailed cat in a rocking chair factory.

It must be Menopause Monday. Do you yell at Donna and tell her not to mess with the thermostat? No! Do you tell her children are ice-skating in the lobby? No! Do you angrily point out that she is changing the climate of Florida? *Hell, no!*

You don your ski parka and mittens and play ice hockey with the kids until it passes. She might feel bad she froze the goldfish but will be a happy, productive employee.

LIFE LESSON ─────────────────────────

The truth is stretchable, so always be kind.

───────────────────────────── DON'T SUCK

TROMBONE

"The only thing that ultimately matters is to eat an ice-cream cone, play a slide trombone, plant a small tree, good God, now you're free."

—RAY MANZAREK

It was 1992, a presidential election year: Clinton versus Bush. The tiny state of New Hampshire is the first in the nation for the presidential primary, so the state was buzzing with activity.

I was living in this great state, a musician at the time, and knew a slew of other musicians in New Hampshire and the Greater Boston area. I had a band that played weddings and corporate events and an entertainment agency that arranged gigs for musicians.

Campaign organizers always hired a competitor entertainment agency in Manchester, New Hampshire, to provide music for the rallies. I played trombone well enough, and because I lived in New Hampshire, the rival agency called me to play at some rallies. This was serious and a wonderful time to be alive! Each band consisted of four to five musicians, and the gig was to play patriotic music before candidates showed up to deliver their speeches.

Upon arrival, we were ushered into a back room to meet the happy, fun-loving Secret Service guys. Sporting their signature earpieces and dark sunglasses, they had the important job of inspecting our instruments and belongings. "The only pain we can inflict is when we are actually playing," I joked. Not even a smile, but that was OK because we felt like low-level rock stars.

When a candidate was announced, we played "Happy Days Are Here Again" as he made his way to the stage. We played the tune about a thousand times. It was fun, and we were happy to be part of these historic events. We typically wore fake straw hats adorning the candidates' names.

As we pondered the $52,000 yearly Berklee College of Music tuition, we played and played and played. The next night, we usually switched hats. Secret Service agents went through our stuff and tried not to snicker, and the next candidate came in to make his pitch.

We hoped we had the stamina to play the same song for two hours. As a horn player, my lips looked like I had lost a street fight. Hey, Instagram models, forget lip injections—just take up a brass instrument.

We were almost done with the second candidate and were some tired musicians. As we walked from the platform, a rotund, red-faced guy approached us. He was wearing the same hat as we were, but he was fit to be tied. "I saw you guys playing last night for the other candidate. You can't be on both sides. Politics are very important, and you can only support red or blue."

Trying not to laugh in his face, I said, "You have obviously spent a great deal of time at the snack table. The snacks from last night are from the same caterer."

We never gave any thought to the candidates or politics. We were simply happy to have a gig.

LIFE LESSON

Politics are not open for discussion, not even at an election campaign rally.

LINDA/BETTY

"Acting is not an important job in the scheme of things. Plumbing is."

—SPENCER TRACY

In business, as in life, you are always better off if you are memorable. This does not mean you must be famous or well known by everyone in your profession or town—it has more to do with what people think or feel about you.

Are you happy, sad, funny, serious, or just plain unforgettable? Another way to think about this is to ponder how you feel about certain people and why. Think about the ever-pleasant bank teller, the Wicked Witch of the West at the Department of Motor Vehicles, or the mechanic who always has a new joke.

Maybe you are simply a nice and pleasant person, known as a breath of fresh air, which goes to show you can be memorable for virtually nothing. Suffice it to say that it's preferable not to be perceived negatively. To live your best life, nicer is better.

For a few years, my business partners and I had a property management firm in Southwest Florida. Our daily routine included fielding repair requests from tenants and implementing repairs. For each situation, we scheduled the best vendor to take care of the job. We hired lots of vendors.

The office staffers at these companies were lovely people, mostly women. But as I called to schedule vendors, I got the impression the staffers weren't treated very well. They seemed a bit beat up by disrespectful customers.

For our part, we were grateful and thrilled to hire these contractors to do all the crazy jobs that came up. Ever try to snake a "hair rat" out of a shower drain?

I strove to have a fun and light attitude, and it was always well received. One random day when I had to call for a plumber, Linda answered the phone as per usual at this company. Although I'd never actually met Linda, in my mind, she was tall, mid-sixties, with Crystal Gale–length hair, skinny jeans, cowboy boots, a pressed white shirt, and turquoise jewelry—lots of it.

I imagined a neat desk, lots of paperwork, and a computer monitor adorned with only two scribbled sticky notes for important phone numbers. I pegged her as a regular at Piggy's Pork Palace and Kimmy's Asian Acrylic House of Nails. She probably had a giant insulated cup from Mobil on the Run filled with Diet Mountain Dew, as well as photos of family and fish (a Florida thing).

Thirty-five years of smoking Marlboros had given her that 1960s woman-named-Evelyn-in-a-donut-shop voice. You learned quickly not to make her laugh too hard lest she'd break into a wheezing, coughing, choking chortle that would end just this side of a ventilator. She liked her donuts plain and her coffee with extra cream and nine sugars.

And for lunch, she ate two Slim Jims and a Little Debbie snack cake. Dinner was Tuna Helper, canned green beans, and *Wheel of Fortune*.

I really liked Linda. She was somewhat brash and tough but a nice person with a good sense of humor. I was always respectful and did my best to make her chuckle (but not too much—the smoker's cough, you know).

One day, I decided to change her name from Linda to Betty. Betty? Yes, Betty. I just thought she sounded more like a Betty than a Linda.

Andre: "Linda, I have made a decision to change your name to Betty."

Linda: "Mr. LeClair, as long as you pay your bills, you can call me Willie Nelson for all I care. Do you need any plumbing, or are you having a slow day?"

She'd really gotten a kick out of the name change. A few days later, I had to call her about a leaky shower valve...

Linda: "Acme Plumbing, may I help you?"

Andre: "Good morning, Betty."

Linda: "Good morning, Mr. LeClair."

Boom! Linda is Betty. Andre is memorable. Hair rats are gone.

LIFE LESSON ———————————————————————————————————

Make people feel special, and they'll remember you for it.

———————————————————————— DON'T SUCK

(10)

DON'T
SUCK

...AT SOLID FRIENDSHIP

THE BEST

"I did my best, and God did the rest."

—HATTIE MCDANIEL

In the mid-1990s, I hung around with a few Greek musicians who played in Lowell, Massachusetts. They played three nights a week for listening, dancing, and sultry belly dancers.

They had played together for years and years in various configurations, but the "star" was Freddie Elias. Fred was a violinist, a damn good one. When I met him, he was in his eighties. He had played all over the country and had a slew of famous musician friends. Everyone always enjoyed Freddie's interesting and impressive stories.

A mutual musician friend introduced him to me, and we were instantly old friends. He had a killer smile and giant hands. He shook my hand and asked if I wanted to do some push-ups. We were in a club full of people, on the dance floor, but I felt compelled to go along with this crazy old man. He easily did more push-ups than I could, even though he was almost fifty years older. I did my best, but more importantly, I was "made." I was hanging out with Freddie Elias! It was epic.

That night started a relationship that lasted until Freddie passed away well into his late 90s. We were brothers.

Freddie had a call list. If you made the list, you might get random calls at any time of the day or night. From his well-worn flip phone, Freddie graced you with his soothing, baritone voice. From current events to old jokes, it was always a pleasure. Every time the guys went to dinner, everyone got a call from Freddie...one by one. Freddie was calling. It was glorious!

Freddie and I lived a town apart in southern New Hampshire, so we got together on his off nights. We had many dinners in "the booth" at CJ's Great West Grill, a restaurant in Manchester, New Hampshire—baked haddock, mashed potatoes, butternut squash, and hot fudge sundaes. Oh, and coffee...*always* coffee. The waitstaff and managers loved him. He walked through the restaurant, shaking hands and smiling! He remembered everyone's name, and they were thrilled.

When we settled in, he called five or six people on the call list, and then he and I traded stories about musicians, music, and life. He told me the same stories every time, and I told him the same jokes, and we both loved it!

I can vividly envision the place, the booth, and Freddie, always dressed up with three shirts, two vests, and a suit coat, even in the summer. It was always warm and comfortable to be around Freddie. I had deep respect and love for this great WWII veteran and hero. It was an honor to join him for those dinners, and I have wonderful everlasting memories.

I had the privilege of calling him my friend. He made everyone feel special, and everyone knew Freddie. He was always interested and engaged, and he never left his home without his million-dollar smile. Every woman he encountered was as beautiful as a flower in a garden, and every guy the most handsome on earth. His unofficial mission was to make everyone feel good. He accomplished that mission brilliantly.

He was *the best*, and he became the best by telling everyone *they* were the best. It was so beautifully simple. He was pure love. An exceptionally talented violinist and accomplished musician, Frederick G. Elias was revered, respected, and loved.

Freddie always said to me, "Brother Andre, you should be a writer." Life is funny. Thanks for being our friend, Brother Fred. We sure do miss you.

LIFE LESSON ───────────────────────

You are the best, and honor your friends!

─────────────────────────── DON'T SUCK

I KNOW AL

"Don't confuse fame with success. Madonna is one; Helen Keller is the other."

—ERMA BOMBECK

In just about every town in America, there are wildly successful restaurants, many owned and operated by a single restaurateur or maybe a family. New England had quite a few:

- Hilltop Steak House, owner Frank Giuffrida
- Anthony's Pier 4, owner Anthony Athanas
- Kowloon, owners the Wong family
- Princeton Lounge, owner Bob White...and many, many more.

I always thought name-dropping was a fascinating dynamic. It has so many levels. There are people who know famous people and people who kind of think they do. Then you have the folks who know local "celebrities" and people who really don't know them.

I find this last category to be the most entertaining. On a local level, the name-droppers are convinced they know people they really can't verify knowing. They don't usually get called out because their friends tend to do the same thing. Local celebrity types might include car dealers with flashy commercials, newscasters, weather forecasters, the wealthy society page people, and of course, popular restaurant owners.

During my nightclub and lounge music days, I spent a lot of time in a particular Chinese restaurant. The owner's name was Al. Al became somewhat of a celebrity by rubbing elbows with his restaurant patrons. Al is a good friend, and we worked together for years until he retired. Al was a brilliant businessman and restaurateur.

Al instinctively knew that as a "celebrity," knowing his guests' names and other details about them was crucial. "Hey, Bill, how's the family? Did you buy a new truck? Is your kid out of prison yet?"

Al was always dressed to the nines. He knew everyone. He was the first person you saw as you entered, and if he knew you, he said hello to you by name, smiled, and asked a question. Some guests wanted to chat, while others just said hello and jumped into a Scorpion Bowl, but you always felt good in his place because that is how he made you feel. He understood people, and it was his secret to success.

Years after he retired and closed the restaurant, I was at a party, reminiscing about all the great restaurants and clubs in New England. Someone recognized me as a karaoke host. I felt very famous! I pretended I recognized him and praised him for his exceptional singing. As we chatted, he shared that he had been a regular at the lounge and knew Al.

I wondered if Al actually knew this patron. I am guessing he did, and I bet Al was thankful the guy's mai tai habit put his kids through college. Al knew the guy, but did the guy know Al? It was brilliant. Al made patrons feel important, and the patrons made Al rich.

I worked for Al for many years and consider him a friend. He always called me "LeClair" and referred to me as his American son. I can boldly say I know Al.

I learned a lot about life from my mentor Al.

LIFE LESSON ————————————————————————

Share what you know with the people
you cherish.

———————————————————————— DON'T SUCK

MENTOR

"It's been true in my life that when I've needed a mentor, the right person shows up."

—KEN BLANCHARD

I am truly fortunate to have had a few mentors in my life.

In 1984, I decided to pursue a life of fame and fortune. I formed a Top 40 dance band to play clubs in the United States and Canada. We rehearsed for a few weeks, and as soon as we had a sound system and two vans, we hit the road.

We played hotel lounges in New England, New York, Ohio, and Pennsylvania. The band was well received, and we had fun. I wasn't getting rich or famous, but that would certainly come soon.

While we were in New York, an agent called to ask if we'd like to play some clubs in Canada. We could not say yes fast enough.

Life as international superstars was grueling but fun. The "tour" was quite glamorous and only eight weeks long. Luckily, our fame enabled us to secure some bookings back in the United States. As soon as the Canada dates ended, we were scheduled to play at a Chinese restaurant lounge in Haverhill, Massachusetts. At the time, Haverhill was on track to be the next Las Vegas, or so we were told.

We had an exceedingly long drive ahead of us, and we had to play that night in the Fortune Cookie Lounge. We traveled in two vans filled with our sound system and seven guys. We were traveling down the Maine Turnpike, and it was rainy and gloomy. We pulled over to switch drivers when the van I was in careened down an embankment and smashed into the rock wall below.

I had been sitting in the passenger seat with my feet on the dashboard. The driver jumped out and ran up the hill to get help. My ankle was throbbing and felt sprained. I hobbled up the muddy hill and walked out onto the highway. I waved my arms like a lunatic. All I could think of was that we had to get to a gig in a few hours.

Finally, a kind driver stopped to help. I jumped in his truck and begged him to take me to the local U-Haul center. This was life before cell phones. The Good Samaritan drove me to the U-Haul center. I rented a truck and drove back to the musicians.

They could not believe we were continuing, but they transferred the gear to the U-Haul, and we were "off like a prom dress."

We arrived in time to set up and started playing right on time at 9:00 p.m. The three customers at the bar seemed to really like the band. My ankle was the size of my career delusion, but we played until 1:00 a.m.

The next day, I called the New England agent to report that we traveled back from Canada and started his gig on time. I also told him about the "Canadian, Sprained Ankle, U-Haul tour." He was extremely impressed that we would play the gig under those circumstances. I appreciated his compliments, but I'd never even considered canceling the gig.

The agent offered me a sales job in his company. I would book bands and DJs for weddings and corporate events. I had always been interested in the business side of music, so I jumped at the opportunity. I dissolved the Top 40 road band and sold the equipment and the van. Come to think of it, we left the other van on the Maine Turnpike. I wonder if it's still there.

I started a wedding band I would book through the agency. The sales position was a blast, and I made boatloads of money. This life adjustment suggestion through my mentor was the key to several great careers in business. He saw something in me I didn't even know was there. Tom is still my mentor and a great friend.

I am an advocate of mentoring and am grateful for my many mentors over the years. In my business life, I have had the honor of mentoring several people with outstanding and life-changing results.

LIFE LESSON

Find a mentor; be a mentor.

DON'T SUCK

11

DON'T
SUCK

...AT BUSINESS TRANSACTIONS

JUICY FRUIT

"I spent every bit of my money to try and get a Mickey Mantle card, and I don't have one. Growing up in Oklahoma, Mickey Mantle was my idol. And here I am, and I'd go pick cotton to have enough money, and I'd buy all of these packs, and I'd chew all of the gum, and I'd never find a Mickey Mantle card."

—JOHNNY BENCH

Life in the fourth grade went along nicely for me as a young boy. We lived in a beautiful house with a swimming pool, my parents worked hard, and life was great on Newfield Street. I was a good kid but didn't really want to hang with the other kids. I did OK in school, but I was distracted by thoughts of being an adult and making money. I spent time alone so I could figure it all out, and then one day, it hit me.

We lived close to the elementary school, so my siblings and I were "walkers." This was kind of sucky on rainy days and in winter, but it toughened us up. The rest of the students had to take the bus. I could walk to a store; they couldn't. They wanted candy and couldn't buy any. I could.

One day, I grabbed some cash from my sock drawer and walked to the store. I had the brilliant idea of specializing in gum. I took an old necktie box and filled it—Wrigley's Spearmint, Doublemint, Juicy Fruit, Clark's Teaberry...whatever they had!

Gum cost me five cents per pack and would easily sell for twice that at school. I discovered I could get a lot of packs in a tie box, and it fit under my arm among my books.

I could barely sleep. I was ten years old.

I got to school the next day, my gum hidden. I had told some key sugar-freaks in advance that I would have the product so they would bring money.

Recess! Many of the boys went to play kickball, and most of the girls were socializing. I took my place on the side of the building and opened the box. It was like shooting fish in a barrel—first day, *sold out.*

The next day and the day after and the day after that...sold out. This was unbelievable to me, and then Willy McDonald came by. Willy wanted to sell SweeTarts and was full of questions. I told him it was a great business but that he needed to find another place to sell. This was *my* area. So that little punk went to the principal and ratted on me. I was shut down immediately, and Willy was, as well, before he even started. Evidently, entrepreneurial kids aren't supposed to sell things at school.

The next thing I knew, I was sitting in the principal's office. Principal Wiggins was a short, serious, chubby, well-organized man who was too tall for his hair. He wore a white shirt and tie and had a desk the size of Texas. I had never been in his office before, but I was the most wanted criminal that day.

He just stared at me. His fat face glistened with sweat as he was angry that he might miss lunch period. "I called your parents, and they are on their way, Mr. LeClair." His formality appealed to me, but my parents weren't going to be pleased.

My mother, Nancy LeClair, was a music teacher in an adjacent town and a classical pianist. She was accomplished, hardworking, *very* well-loved, no-nonsense, a bit sassy, and a lot of fun...unless you wasted her time. She taught school during the day and after-school piano lessons at our house, so she had very little spare time.

She blasted past Wiggins's secretary and into his office. She gave me a loving look as if to say, "Why am I here?"

"Mrs. LeClair, your son has been caught selling gum to the other students."

"Principal Wiggins, if that is against the rules, he will never do it again." She turned to me, smiled, and marched out of the office.

Gulp...one down, one to go.

My father, Bob LeClair, was vice president of a printing company and a part-time singer (a really good one). Bob was classy, pleasant, a super salesman, smart, very well loved, funny as hell, respectful, and old-school.

"Mr. LeClair, we caught your son selling gum to the other students."

Papa was digging this. He sat down next to me, gave me a big smile, and said, "Principal Wiggins, I assume that selling gum in school is against the rules, and he will not do it again. However, I am very proud of him, and you should be as well. Andre is a good boy and does well in school. For some reason, he was born an adult and has an entrepreneurial spirit that frankly fascinates the family. He will be very successful someday because he has heart and soul and works like an animal. By the way, I really like your tie."

Then Dad winked at me and said, "See you later, Sunny. We are taking you out to dinner tonight."

I felt proud, blessed, and lucky. But I was still in the Wiggins chamber. "You have great parents. Don't sell gum anymore, and get out of here."

We shook hands, and I uttered, "Yessir."

As I walked out, he yelled, "Get me Willy McDonald."

LIFE LESSON

Follow the rules, and honor your parents.

UNBELIEVABLE

"It's unbelievable how much you don't know about the game you've been playing all your life."

—MICKEY MANTLE

OK, here is where it all begins. When people meet, they are quite interested in the status of the other person. It usually goes something like this...

John: "Hey, Brian, how are you?"

Brian: "Good, and you?"

John: "Great and yourself?"

I'm not entirely sure why the question is asked three times, but now that you've read this, you will be painfully aware of it. The point is that we all ask and tell our statuses...all day, every day.

"How you doin'?"

"Fine."

"Wassup?"

"Not much."

You constantly meet new people and reconnect with others you already know. Your greeting is your calling card. What better way to make a perfect first impression?

In business, your greeting defines you. Big smile, firm handshake, and proudly state your name and company. You may also elect to go a bit over the top by offering a tagline: "Hi, I'm Sally with Sunshine Real Estate, and you might get *burned* if you don't call me."

Goofy? Yes, but memorable. You could also wear a name tag, so prospective clients have an even better chance of remembering you. This is not for everyone, but I strongly encourage name tags for realtors. As a Realtor, I never wore one.

My ~~friend~~ brother Curtis is an ultra-successful Realtor in Massachusetts. Engaging and enthusiastic, this guy is always in a great mood. He is a branding legend and has his company name on everything he wears. He understands how to present himself, and his customers are raving fans. He is inspiring. He is unbelievable.

I attended a sales seminar many years ago, and one of the speakers, Tom Hopkins, had a great idea. He lamented how he observed that most people, when asked how they are doing, respond with an uninspiring or ho-hum answer. "Be professional, enthusiastic, and excited!" he exclaimed.

When someone asks how you are, look them in the eye, smile your biggest and best smile, and answer, "Unbelievable!"

As Tom Hopkins says, "because it covers it either way."

Be unbelievable, be fun, and be successful.

SILLY WABBIT

"Always make the audience suffer as much as possible."
—ALFRED HITCHCOCK

In my hit-or-miss business life, we always tried unconventional and interesting ways to market.

The wedding business is filled with emotional women we lovingly refer to as "brides." After you work weddings for so many years, you come to realize that once a woman becomes a bride-to-be, she suddenly shifts to a new life form that's a force of nature—admittedly not all women but quite a few of them, based on my experience.

The challenge was that in order to part brides from their new-found riches (read: wedding budgets), we had to be unique, fun, charming, professional, and expensive, of course—sort of like dating without an ending. When booking a wedding, we sent some form of media, such as a videotape or CD, along with documents like a playlist, reception checklists, and so on.

Sometimes we added some unique items—candy, heart-shaped magnets, sunglasses, pens, mouse pads, and other logo-printed items. One day, I had a great idea.

I remembered that as a kid, we had lucky rabbit-foot keychains. I researched and found I could buy these things by the gross (144 to be exact) and in assorted colors! Each plastic toy actually felt like the boney, fur-covered foot of a rabbit. This was of no concern to me, as I was solely interested in the marketing value.

My idea was launched, and the first few brides called to confirm they'd received their packets of information. Then they asked about the rabbit's foot key chain, quite curious as to why we'd sent it.

"We sent you a lucky rabbit's foot in case you hire another band," we told the brides. I was so proud of this brilliant and funny response. Who needs Marketing 101?

We had fun with the nutty idea until bridezilla Jennifer called to say she was appalled to find the foot of a dead rabbit in her promotional package. *Oh, boy. Think fast, Andre.*

"The neon green rabbit never even missed his left front foot. He was still able to hop along on one foot rather joyfully." Jennifer was not amused. "No plastic rabbits were killed in the promotion of this musical group." Silence. At least I wasn't marrying Jennifer, and this was a fun exchange, but...

Jennifer was mortified and demanded an apology for the tasteless and horrifying "stunt." She went on to say that since we were mean to animals, we were not the type of band she wanted performing at her $100,000 wedding reception.

As of this writing, I have 138 rabbit feet stored in my garage.

LIFE LESSON ─────────────────────────────────────

Funny isn't funny to everyone, so know your audience.

── DON'T SUCK

NO SUBSTITUTIONS

"Southwest Airlines is successful because the company understands it's a customer service company. It also happens to be an airline."

—HARVEY MACKAY

One of the businesses we got involved in was karaoke—yes, karaoke! Karaoke was huge in Asia, then in Hawaii, then on the West Coast, then the East Coast, and then our neck of the woods, New England. Ours was one of the first entertainment companies in the area to offer karaoke.

Karaoke was a smashing success for the clubs and karaoke companies, and a blast for singing patrons. It proved to be a right-place-at-the-right-time scenario, although it was a bit of a gamble for me.

At the time, I was dead broke, divorced, overweight, and going through foreclosure and bankruptcy. I was quite the eligible bachelor. I was anxious to get my life on track and build back my finances, and it seemed karaoke was my ticket.

I had *no* money, so I sold my car to buy my first system. I also bought an old broken-down van that smelled like charcoal from the fire damage it sustained. I booked myself at a Chinese restaurant for a six-week trial run. We decided Thursdays would be best.

I had a poster made for the lobby, printed the songlist books and song request slips, and even got golf pencils for the drunken singers to make their selections. I was ready!

Karaoke night took off, and within a short time, we were at capacity every week. I wore a suit and tie, just like the owner, and tried to be a fun and accommodating host. It was a fun gig, and I made money to reinvest in the business by buying more systems. It was a crazy time. At the end of every night during those early days of my karaoke career, I personally thanked every person in the club. I was grateful to have a job, and if I treated patrons right, I would continue to be employed.

And so it went—Thursday night karaoke. The gig lasted for years and years, continuing long after I retired the vodka-soaked suit and tie. Many of the waitresses and bartenders worked Thursday nights with me for years. We formed lasting friendships and had a lot of fun together.

We longed for brighter days when we would never again have to hear anyone sing "The Rose" or "American Pie" (eight minutes and forty-two seconds, by the way). Making fun of the singers practically became an art form, and we drank until we dulled our senses, especially our hearing.

One bartender asked to sing. He was a decent singer, but to keep him humble, we said, "As a singer, you are a very good bartender!" We became friends as we were both interested in buying rental properties and making money.

One night after the patrons were gone, he asked to talk. He said he had observed me from the first night and for hundreds of nights after that. He wanted to share his thoughts, which ended up being a valuable life lesson for me.

In broken English, he said, "LeClair, when you first started, you would say goodbye and thank everyone in the club at the end of the night. You had no money and would eat rolls and butter in the kitchen for dinner. I watched everything you did for years. I could see you were working hard, building your business, and becoming more successful by the week.

"Now you have a booming karaoke business, a second home in Florida, and a BMW. And now, instead of thanking the patrons at the end of the night, you pack up the system, and you sneak out the back door. Because you have money in your pocket, you no longer care about the people that gave you the money."

I politely thanked my friend, but I was rocked. *Who do I think I am?* I thought. His point was well taken. I'd gone from being broke to being successful, and I'd forgotten how I got there. I vowed never to act that way again. I was appreciative of his observations and friendship.

LIFE LESSON

There is *no* substitute for an attitude of gratitude.

DON'T SUCK

IT'S NOT ABOUT YOU

"To be successful in real estate, you must always and consistently put your clients' best interests first. When you do, your personal needs will be realized beyond your greatest expectations."

—ANTHONY HITT

Being a Realtor is not rocket science, but there is a lot to learn, and the more knowledge you have, the more successful you will become. It is also very important to have mentors and friends to help you along the way.

As our real estate business grew in Sarasota, we were involved in more sales transactions. I had come from the rental management side and had been involved in sales transactions, but not in Florida. We had listed a two-bedroom condo unit, and a local broker had a buyer. The deal went on to close without a hitch.

During a meeting in my office with Brian, the buyer's broker, I realized just how knowledgeable and competent he was. He was also one of the funniest guys I had ever met, and since I always have a difficult time being serious, we were destined to be great friends.

We have been friends for years, and during our marathon dinners, we chat about all things real estate. With any extra time, we solve all the world's problems. Brian is my real estate mentor, and over the years, he has been truly generous with his time and knowledge.

Every single time we discuss real estate, he says the same thing: "It's not about you."

"But I know more about real estate than the sellers."

"It's not about you."

"They should be happy with the strong offer."

"It's not about you."

"They are leaving money on the table."

"It's not about you."

"Their asking price is way too high."

"It's not about you."

His point is very well-taken and one of the many reasons he is an extremely successful real estate broker. This philosophy is very sound advice in almost any business. Whether your business is houses, cars, or copper pipes, it's not about you. You are not selling; you are helping customers buy.

When someone hires you, it's always about them and never about you!

LIFE LESSON

Get over yourself and serve your customers.

DON'T SUCK

12

DON'T
SUCK

...AT TIME MANAGEMENT

EARLY BIRD SPECIAL

"The early bird may get the worm, but it's the second mouse that gets the cheese."

—JEREMY PAXMAN

In my humble opinion, being late is obnoxious and rude. Everyone has had experiences with chronically late people, and we secretly— or not so secretly—hate their guts. I certainly do.

I'm convinced the chronically late are self-important, attention-starved, or not too bright. They have old worn-out excuses for being late that are usually lies, so when they are actually late due to a legitimate reason, they become the boy who cried wolf.

When you are chronically late, you are known as the "late guy." As the late guy, you miss opportunities because the world hates you. You also stop getting invited to parties and events because everyone hates you. Why be hated?

Even people who are "fashionably late" are secretly hated. Actually, we are jealous that they are so successful at being as late as they want, but I digress.

TIME

Time is a commodity. You can't buy more, and you can never get it back once it's gone. Whether you are the president or a street person, we all have the same twenty-four hours in a day.

We had an employee who was always late for work. It seemed her car was prone to traffic jams and accidents. She used the driving excuse so many times her nickname was "Five-Car Pileup" and, eventually, simply "Five-Car." She wasn't thrilled about the nickname, but she continued to be late, so it stuck.

In your personal or business life, you do a disservice to yourself if you are habitually late. All the people affected by your royal lateness don't perceive you as important. They see your face as a dartboard. They are not fans of your behavior and will eventually cross you off the invite list.

WEDDED BLISS?

There is one accepted exception to time etiquette. It's called Bride Time. If you have attended a few weddings, perhaps you've noticed the bride is *never* on time.

Here's how the clever wedding industry sells "lateness." You receive an invitation to John and Susie's wedding. The ceremony is set for 6:00 p.m. You arrive at 5:45 so you can get a good seat, and everyone can check out your snazzy wedding outfit.

Six p.m. comes and goes. The tension builds. Where the heck is Bridezilla?

It's 6:15. *All rise.* Time for holy matrimony—the walk, the vows, the rings, the pronouncing of husband and wife, the kiss, a huge round of applause, and...it's 6:30, which happens to be the exact start time of cocktail hour. Magic, right? Nope.

Actually, the wedding industry has figured out a way to merge lateness with being on time, and voila! So unless you are shopping for wedding gowns, please develop the habit of being on time *all* the time.

To go one better, be early! This is an overlooked power play that's easy to pull off.

REAL ESTATE

In real estate, usually, two realtors are involved in showings, closings, open houses, and so on. Think about it—the early Realtor is relaxing on the property while the other is late, frazzled, and sweating because he doesn't understand the concept of time management.

Which Realtor is more impressive in the eyes of the clients —early, calm Realtor or frazzled, sweaty Realtor? Be early; be successful.

For those who think this is simply common sense, pay attention to how others handle time management. It's an incredibly easy way to have an edge in your business and in life, so do it!

HUNGRY?

As we age, apparently, we are genetically programmed to eventually want dinner at 3:00 p.m. If you are so inclined (and you will be), you can go to a restaurant and get some wonderful bargain-priced culinary delights called Early Bird Specials. If you like to eat dinner right after lunch, this is a great benefit of being a senior citizen.

Don't be late, because after 5:00, the specials end and it is time to feed the normal people.

LIFE LESSON

Fifteen minutes early is late for the truly punctual.

DON'T SUCK

TIMING

"The secret to modern life is finding the measure in time management. I have two kids, a career, and I travel, and I don't think my life is any different than most couples. The most valuable commodity now for many people is time and how to parcel that out."

—HUGH JACKMAN

What's the secret to good...timing? Comedy.

Everyone seems to be rushed in this ultrafast-paced world. A world of information is instantly available at our fingertips. We spend more time deciding what to order on Uber Eats than we would preparing dinner. Have we lost our perspective on time?

It seems we are woefully unaware of the time it takes to complete certain tasks. Unfortunately, this unawareness causes us to avoid doing things that should be done. By not doing necessary tasks, we become stressed and frustrated.

The solution is actually quite easy. The secret is knowing the amount of time it takes to complete certain tasks.

EXAMPLE #1: GLASS SHOWER DOORS

If you have glass shower doors and you never take the time to clean them, eventually, you will feel like you are taking a shower in a snowstorm—a disgusting soap-buildup wintery wonderland. You would think an area that has gallons of water and various soaps would be the cleanest place in the house, but soap scum is tough stuff.

Here's the good news: a wonderful cleaning device is available—the squeegee. If you get a wetsuit, a timer, and a squeegee, you will discover that cleaning shower doors takes about twenty-two seconds. Yes, twenty-two seconds to squeegee your fancy glass doors after every shower is worth it.

Snow globes are meant for miniature reindeer and ice skaters.

EXAMPLE #2: ONE-MINUTE TASKS

Once you realize how long a minute is, you will be amazed at what you can accomplish. In the time it takes to microwave a Hot Pocket, you can do the following:

- Water your plants.
- Wash some dishes in the sink.
- Sing "Happy Birthday" to a friend or two.

EXAMPLE #3: BOILING WATER

As the saying goes, "a watched pot never boils." It does boil, but it takes a very long time. Or does it? Instead of standing and watching the rigatoni boil to death, do something:

- Dance erotically to "Superstition" by Stevie Wonder.
- Stalk your past lovers on Facebook.
- Clean the cobwebs out of the ceiling fan that have been there since 1998.
- Make love—this will add a few seconds but is worth it, plus rigatoni for afterward!

Once you realize making your bed won't take eight minutes, you will make it every single day, maximizing your time and creating a neat and orderly living space.

So, vacuum your car, send a note to Aunt Milly, fold your socks, and floss your teeth.

We will all benefit.

LIFE LESSON ————————————————————————

Make the most of your time.

——————————————————————— DON'T SUCK

PLANES, TRAINS, AND BOREDOM IN SEAT 7C

"I don't know where I'm going from here, but I promise it won't
be boring."

—DAVID BOWIE

The more successful you become, the more you will be on airplanes.

People fly places. They fly for business, they fly to visit family,
and they fly to vacation destinations. They rack up frequent-flier
miles, and then they fly some more. Flying is a wonderful time to
catch up on resting and, more important, reading.

Air travel is great—no cell phone use, light snacks, drinks, and
enthusiastic attendants who appear at the push of a button. What's
not to love? Air travel affords a unique opportunity to get places fast.

Some flights are short in duration, but others last for many,
many hours. It's a great time to read. Someone else is driving, and the
flight deck is locked, so you couldn't fly the plane if you wanted to.

Read, read, and read! Skip the in-flight magazine that's loaded
with ads, and instead, read something fun or meaningful or at least
work-related.

We have all witnessed the bored guy on a plane. He is on his way
to some discount vacation with "the wife." (By the way, when refer-
ring to a wife, "the" isn't the term I'd suggest to set her apart from
all the other wives.) He sits and sighs, fiddling with the snack food
package. He sucks.

He is not using his time wisely. He doesn't realize that even sleeping is a better use of time than staring at the back of the seat and wondering how long until landing. Don't be this guy.

Get a novel or trade journal, or better yet, read this book, *DON'T SUCK*. Reading on a plane is a gift from the aviation gods. You have a substantial amount of uninterrupted quiet time, and you will be smarter when you land.

Buy some books to keep in your carry-on, and travel the world! You will be glad you did.

THE FRIENDLY SKIES

Along with doing nothing and reading a book lies the concept of conversation (not recommended, however). You could strike up a conversation with your seatmates, but more than likely, they do not want to talk to you. Even worse, they do want to talk to you, and they are uninteresting and boring. And to make matters worse, it's bad form to fall asleep while someone is chatting with you.

You could consider starting a polite conversation only to discover it eventually times out. Unfortunately, you cannot say you are late for an appointment unless you have a parachute, and then it is awkward silence with 679 miles to Cleveland.

Sadly—or luckily for some—we are a text-obsessed society, and people really do not want to chat. They want to look at their phones every minute of every day. Eventually, we will all be hunchbacks.

If you are very advanced, chat up the flight attendant. If you make a love connection and get married, you travel for free. This is much better than reading.

Read books—it will improve your life.

13

DON'T
SUCK

...AT PROPER ETIQUETTE

THANK YOU

"If the only prayer you ever say in your entire life is thank you, it will be enough."

—MEISTER ECKHART

Do chickens smile? At Chick-fil-A, they seem to—well, the employees do anyway. This fast-food chicken chain has been deemed the most polite chain in the restaurant business, according to industry reports. Chick-fil-A employees don't do anything Earth-shaking to earn the chain these rankings—they simply say "please" and "thank you" and smile at drive-thru customers.

Publix Super Markets is another example. When you shop at Publix and need assistance, a polite team member cheerfully answers your question or guides you through the store. When you thank them for their assistance, the wonderful store staffers are trained to reply, "It's my pleasure."—not "yup," not "sure," not a grunt, and not "you're welcome," which makes no sense anyway. (*You're welcome?* Welcome to what?) Good job, Publix!

My personal favorite is "no worries." It goes down like this: You are in a store. You accidentally bump into a person. You feel bad and say "excuse me" or "sorry." The guy usually says, "Hey, dude, no worries." *Dude?* I didn't realize I was on a ranch, nor that he had the ability to dramatically alter my life. "No worries." This is just wonderful! Is this for the rest of the day, week, or month? Does it time out? It may even be for the rest of my life—what great luck. I can innocently bump into a cowboy, and for the rest of my days, I am worry free. Take *that*, Publix!

While I am at it, what is with the weird use of the word "right"? For a while, it was "yeah, right," and then it was changed to saying it with the inflection on "right" ("yeah, *right?*"), but *now* the "yeah" is gone. Now when you agree with someone or something, you smile and nod and say, "Right?" You express agreement by saying a word—very efficiently—in the form of a question. Here is an example:

You: "Hey, Gertrude, it's hot in here."

Gertrude: "Right?"

Who thinks this stuff up, and why do we follow that person?

LIFE LESSON ⎯⎯⎯⎯⎯⎯⎯⎯⎯⎯⎯⎯⎯⎯⎯⎯⎯⎯⎯⎯⎯⎯⎯⎯⎯

Mind your manners.

⎯⎯⎯⎯⎯⎯⎯⎯⎯⎯⎯⎯⎯⎯⎯⎯⎯⎯⎯⎯⎯⎯⎯⎯⎯⎯⎯⎯ DON'T SUCK

KNIFE AND FORK

"I don't stop eating when I'm full. The meal isn't over when I'm full. It's over when I hate myself."

—LOUIS C. K.

Unless you are still in college and eat only pizza, correctly handling utensils is a very big deal. This is a simple skill that will serve you well in your adult life. I have seen too many folks hold a knife and a fork as if all the bones in their hands were broken.

If none of this makes sense to you, and you feel it doesn't matter how the food gets from the plate to your mouth, you might consider enrolling in charm school or living on pizza forever.

My father was a stickler about this, and at the time, I thought he was being ridiculous. At Sunday dinner, while I was drooling over the roast beef, Mr. French was teaching me how to properly use a knife and fork. The beef was perfectly medium-rare, so I was a fast learner. Dad was a cool and classy guy, and I am eternally grateful.

Since we are on the subject, *please* do not cut your food into cubes. There are only two times in life when this is allowed: The first time is when you are a toddler. The next time is...*never*. If you are dedicated to cubing your chow, I suggest you also add a baseball cap (worn backward) and chew with your mouth open.

When you are invited to weddings, special dinners, and business meetings, if you don't want to see other guests roll their eyes, you need to refine these skills. This is one of the easiest ways to rise above the crowd and be a classy, sophisticated human, so get on it.

The best way to understand table manners that are as juvenile as Bamm-Bamm Rubble's is to observe restaurant patrons. Any restaurant that serves food requiring a knife and fork will do. Start at the local diner, graduate to a neighborhood restaurant, and then when you feel confident, go to an expensive steak house.

You will be impressed and shocked. You will see people who can't afford to be there with great table manners and ultrawealthy who may as well be fed by a nurse. Money doesn't necessarily equal class, but it's fun to see the struggle. If millions of people can work chopsticks, how hard can it be to manage a fork and knife? (I have never used chopsticks but have wondered what you do about soup.)

Once you master the basic knife and fork, you will be at a dinner party and realize how inept people look. You will be thrilled you don't suck, people will adore you, and you will become very wealthy.

You will also no longer be a fool.

LIFE LESSON

Toothpicks are for later, elbows off the table, and leave the sugar packets.

DON'T SUCK

TIPPING IS NOT A CITY IN CHINA

"I didn't want to be short. I've tried to pretend that being a short guy didn't matter. I tried to make up for being short by affecting a strut, by adopting the voice of a much bigger man, by spending more money than I made, by tipping double or triple at bars and restaurants, by dating tall, beautiful women."

—MICKEY ROONEY

In the early 1980s, I attended Berklee College of Music in Boston, Massachusetts. At the time, stage parents considered it to be Berklee Bank and Trust. School administrators sat prospective students at a piano and asked them to play increasingly more difficult music. Once a student's ability was determined, the next step was the finance office.

Delusional singers and guitar players arrived en masse. The stage parents spared no expense, paying for the future Britney Spears or Stevie Ray Vaughn in hopes of multimillion-dollar record contracts and early retirement.

To be fair, really good musicians could become great, but even if you were a below-average musician who was very well received at family functions, Berklee had a tuition bill for you too.

And not mentioned publicly was the unofficial Berklee College of Alcohol. I was enrolled in this program along with a handful of other gifted musicians.

Most of our study happened off campus, but our tuition money was as green as our morning complexions, so we were tolerated. Showing up is 90 percent? We were 100 percent no-show for classes. Heck, it wasn't law school. We were already playing clubs a few nights a week, so the music classes didn't seem to make any sense.

While we readied our livers to donate to Tufts University School of Medicine, one of us actually became a very serious musician. Ozzie was a skinny kid from Long Island, New York. Although he and I were trombone majors, he actually practiced and studied music. My trombone stayed safe and sound, nestled in its case, where it is to this day.

Ozzie became one of the best trombone players in the world, touring with major groups and entertainers for years. He is truly a gifted, talented, hardworking musician. We were very good friends at Berklee but lost touch over the years.

Fast-forward thirty-plus years and Ozzie called me to sell his parents' home in Florida. As luck would have it, his parents lived in Sarasota, where I had a real estate firm. This was crazy! So, we met at a local place to reconnect.

I couldn't believe I was seeing my pal Ozzie after all those years. I rarely have expectations, but I wondered what he was like and was excited to see him. Our reunion was epic. We reminisced about our Berklee days and caught up on what we were now doing. It was just fantastic. We were both loud due to being half deaf from playing music for so many years, but it was so cool.

We laughed and laughed, and we were amazed it had been forty years since we had last seen each other. Four decades had passed, and we were still twenty-year-old punks. We laughed so hard we got right to the edge of damaging our spleens. I'm sure there is a name for this medical condition, but the laughter and joy outweighed any potential spleen injuries.

At one point, the waitress told us she had to leave and that we would have another waitress. Ozzie said, "Bring the tab, please, and have the other waitress start a new tab so we can make sure you receive your tip."

I have always respected and appreciated restaurant staff, as their job is difficult and mostly unappreciated. Ozzie felt the same, and we took good care of both waitresses. I wasn't sure after all the years what he would be like, but he is a classy, talented, and beautiful guy, and I am proud to be his friend.

LIFE LESSON ⎯⎯⎯⎯⎯⎯⎯⎯⎯⎯⎯⎯⎯⎯⎯

Take care of the waitstaff by tipping big.

⎯⎯⎯⎯⎯⎯⎯⎯⎯⎯⎯⎯⎯ DON'T SUCK

（14）

DON'T SUCK

SUCK

...AT BEING YOURSELF

NEVER SAY SHOULD

"I always wanted to be somebody, but now I realize I should have been more specific."

—LILY TOMLIN

This is an interesting concept and something that has bothered me for many years.

I believe there are basically two ways one might be inclined to predominantly use the word "should."

You should.

I should.

The goal is to eliminate both phrases from your vocabulary.

EXAMPLE #1: "YOU SHOULD"

You: "John, you *should* date Sally. You are not getting any younger, you are not that handsome, and she actually likes you. She is the perfect girl to settle down with. You *should* be with her."

John: "You *should* keep your opinions to yourself and concentrate on your own life. Not that it matters, because you are obviously an omniscient mystic, but Sally is not only moving to Botswana to join the Peace Corps, but she doesn't wear deodorant and has a dead rat collection."

So much for your uninformed use of the word "should." John does not benefit from your expert advice. Never say, "You should..."

EXAMPLE #2: "I SHOULD"

You: "I *should* go to night school and get my law degree. I also *should* get married, have kids, and buy a house with a picket fence and neighbors who have kids, a swimming pool, and a Land Rover."

Wrong! Follow your dreams, listen to your gut feelings, and make life decisions based on what you *want* to do. Hey, having a law degree, a trophy wife, a few brats, and a neighbor you hate could be a great way to go, but only if it's what you want. When you think you *should* do things, you risk landing on Planet Regret. Never say, "I should."

This *should* be common sense, but good sense is usually anything but common. *Should* I continue?

LIFE LESSON ────────────────────────────────

Mind your own business because you want to, not because you should.

──────────────────────────────── DON'T SUCK

PASSION

"Passion is one great force that unleashes creativity, because if you're passionate about something, then you're more willing to take risks."

—YO-YO MA

There are passionate singers who go to karaoke bars every night. Singing is their passion. They aren't particularly good singers, but their delusion allows them to pretend they will have a career in music. A lot of pretending sometimes comes along with passion.

The karaoke disciples identify themselves as legitimate singers, and as a result, some people think they are wacky. Some karaoke singers look down on their day jobs, so they become stagnant and passed over for promotions.

Fortunately, they get to bask in the warmth of their delusion. As a side note, let me point out that most karaoke singers just want to drink, sing, and have fun. Passionate or not, they are mostly awful singers.

Full disclosure: I made a bundle as a karaoke host.

MARY

Mary did scrapbooking. Mary loved scrapbooking. Mary was passionate about scrapbooking. Mary had many friends who also loved scrapbooking. Mary's car had quilted seat covers.

Mary quit her job as an executive assistant but had a passion for scrapbooking. Mary scrapbooked day and night. Mary lived in a rented double-wide, and Mary was always broke. Mary had two cats: Scrap and Book. Mary's neighbors were alcoholics who pretended to enjoy her scrapbooking if she gave them beer.

Mary made very little money from an early investment, all of which she spent on scrapbooking supplies. Mary lived like a homeless person due to her passion, even though she was an in-demand executive assistant. Mary had made lots of money as an executive assistant since she was very good at her job.

Mary did what she was passionate about but not what she was good at. Mary did not have money, was passionate and delusional, and had only pretend boyfriends.

Most people have dreams of creating a life around their passions, but some are not particularly gifted when it comes to their passions. They might be good at what they do for a living, but they live a life of delusion and make little money.

There are exceptions, but even Tiger Woods does what he is good at, and although it is a passion, hitting practice balls ten hours a day must take some of the shine off the passion. Tiger is a gifted golfer, but professional golf is intense and, in my opinion, a lot less fun than playing mini-golf at Fun-o-Rama.

JOE

Joe played clarinet. Joe loved the clarinet. Joe was passionate about the clarinet. Joe had very few friends due to the clarinet. Joe was a software engineer by day and played clarinet at night. The clarinet was his passion.

Joe lived in a nice house with a nice wife, two good kids, and an aggravating guinea pig named Benny Goodman. Joe's neighbors loved him between songs and plotted his death during polka time.

Joe made good money and was able to pursue his passion because of his job. Joe did what he was good at so he could also do what he was passionate about.

A passion should not break you. If you do what you are good at, you will be able to fund your passion and live a successful life. Reality is always your friend. Your passion could very well turn into your profession, so stay positive and be open to opportunities. Embrace your passion for what it is.

Love your passion, and when the world is ready to embrace it, we will let you know.

LIFE LESSON ——————————————————————————

Never sing "The Greatest Love of All."

DON'T SUCK

IMPROV

"Some of the people I've met in those first few weeks of even trying improv classes are still my friends now—15, 17 years later."

—LAUREN ASH

Studying improv was one the absolute best things I have ever done in my life. I studied in Boston and, years later, in Florida.

There was a very cool improv club in Boston's historic North End neighborhood. Located in a basement directly below a CVS Pharmacy, it was set up as a theater-in-the-round. It was dark and funky, and it was a blast!

After seeing a poster advertising the improv school, I decided to check it out, and it proved to be a great decision. I never had any intention of becoming an improv comedian, but I was drawn to the mystery of being able to make sh** up on the spot.

The first class was made up of six students, and we met every Tuesday night. The class included the following students:

- Homemaker who aspired to be an improv actor
- United Parcel Service driver
- Figure skater
- Biologist
- Certified Public Accountant
- Me

Improv is a complex craft that requires a lot of technique, and it is deeply challenging. Not for the squeamish, it rips you out of your comfort zone and takes you on a scary ride through your psyche, strengths, and weaknesses.

I realized early on that this course ultimately made me fast on my feet, focused, and unflappable. Plus, it came with lots of silly fun and laughs. Scads of games and exercises got the improv students involved and focused.

Although some students were funnier than others, it was not about outdoing one another. It was more about working as part of a team, making good scenes, and trusting my teammates and my instincts.

The entire program was six levels, eight weeks each, and we did a performance at the end of all the classes—on the main stage!

I cannot stress enough the value of improv to up my game in business and in life. I credit much of my success to improv.

Want six great reasons to study improv? Here's what Samantha Jacobs has to say:

1. You'll learn how to think on your feet. This skill is one that will come in handy in the classroom, a work environment, and just day-to-day life. In improv, you can't overthink your reaction, weighing the pros and cons of how you should respond to a situation because you have to act NOW, in the moment while you are on stage. That's what improvisation means! Training yourself to quickly size up a situation, make a choice, and react with confidence is an awesome ability to have (some would say it's a superpower.)

2. You'll learn how to say *yes*. The first rule of improv is to always say yes. Though this may be a fun challenge in the classroom, this skill will help introduce you to things outside of your comfort zone outside of the classroom as well. Let's face it, in life, there are plenty of times when it's easier

to say "No" to a situation. Learning to say "Yes" almost always opens up doors to new experiences and helps you grow and learn new things.

3. You'll laugh...hard. Laughing is good for your soul...and your abs. It releases tension too. Chances are, if you are stressed out about something before your improv class, after a good laugh, you'll feel better about whatever it was that was bothering you.

4. You'll make new friends. Amy Poehler and Tina Fey met in an improv class...just saying. Improv classes require a sense of trust and intimacy. And the no judgment zone helps you to open up and really get to know others and yourself. Professional relationships can flourish as well with friends from an improv class because you know they've got your back. Working together is a logical next step. Trust is key when you're working without a script.

5. You'll improve your public speaking skills. Learning to perform in front of a class will help you to give presentations and speeches in any sort of setting, casual or professional. Research has shown that public speaking is one of the top ten phobias of the general population, yet it is also one of the necessities of life. Training in improv will help you overcome that fear and teaches you to be a more effective speaker in almost any situation. Improv class teaches you to recover from mistakes, learn to laugh at yourself, and put others at ease.

6. You'll become more open-minded. This applies to everything: people, opportunities, risks, etc. Nothing bad will come from a more open mind. Along with gaining a more open mind comes flexibility and a willingness to face difficult situations instead of avoiding them.

As you can see, I could do a commercial to promote improv, but given that almost anyone can easily understand the above-listed six benefits, I strongly recommend looking into it.

LIFE LESSON

Real life is improvisational theater.

DANCE, DANCE, DANCE

"When you dance, your purpose is not to get to a certain place on the floor. It's to enjoy each step along the way."

—WAYNE DYER

Brendon Burchard is a dynamic speaker and a fantastic teacher. He powerfully motivates and inspires audiences across the world. I have read his books, and I am a fan.

In 2019, a friend and I attended the Influencer Convention. It was Brendon's event, but several other great speakers delivered presentations. It was three days of motivation and inspiration, very intense but well worth the effort.

On the first day, the attendees gathered in a grand ballroom. Three thousand people were eager to go, and it was 8:00 a.m. After many years in the music business, 8:00 a.m. felt like 5:00 a.m. to me, but I was ready!

On cue, the house lights faded to black, and bright, flashing, colorful lights and lasers cut through the darkness. The music pumped louder and louder, and the excitement was building.

"Everyone on your feet. Are you ready to be *inspired*?" We were all on our feet. "Ladies and gentlemen, Brendon Burchard!"

The curtain opened at the side of the stage, and Brendon ran out and started dancing. Yes, dancing! *Oh, no...What the—.*

I certainly was not prepared for dancing. I'd spent many years as a musician, making fun of middle-aged men who attempted to dance at weddings, and now I was waving my arms wildly.

I was one of three thousand exuberant dance contestants. As I stopped worrying about how silly I looked, I noticed my leg was moving in a 1965 Elvis kind of way. I felt my top teeth biting into my lower lip, and it felt oddly normal. Who *was* I?

This mental and physical exercise lasted only about two minutes before it was over. Notebooks and pens were out, and it was time to sit down and learn.

Brendon Burchard was a top professional and a brilliant influencer, but more important, he was 100 percent himself. His authentic self danced out on stage, and his authenticity was the catalyst for the contagious dancing.

Admittedly, I was relieved that those I'd danced with were total strangers, and I am guessing many attendees felt the same. But I was personally inspired by Brendon's authenticity and decided to author this book as a result.

If I am ever caught dancing, at least I'll understand why.

Don't just flail your arms—dance!

BE KNOWN

"Somewhere, something incredible is waiting to be known."
—SHARON BEGLEY

We all know lots of people—family, friends, coworkers, and neighbors. We also know of people—restaurant owners, car dealers, and the Rolling Stones. Of course, famous people are known, but no matter who you are, being known is of great importance.

Coincidentally, you are on various lists as well. Everyone you know keeps mental lists, just like you do, and unless you live in a cabin in northern Maine, everyone who knows you *knows* you. They may know the real you, or they may know the fake person you present to them, but trust me, they know some version of you.

So unless you never come out of your basement, the way you are perceived is very important.

We are all too familiar with loudmouthed John, argumentative Jim, or know-it-all Kathy. We know these annoying types, and we don't particularly like them.

On the other hand, we also know helpful Peter, funny Phil, and intelligent Tom. Such folks are wonderful parts of our lives, and we love them—the friendly cashier, the non-creepy car salesperson, and the neighbor with the pickup truck! The key is to be known as the nice, fun, helpful person.

In business, as in your personal life, you know how much you dislike people who suck. This is a reflective hint to you that if you want to be sucky, you will be disliked. You don't need to have a lot going for you if you are pleasant. People will treat you better in return. It's way too easy.

We had an unpleasant experience dealing with a Realtor on a condo sale. The owner was a management client, and we took care of his properties. He decided the market had reached a level where it made sense for him to sell. Due to a language barrier, he hired a Realtor at another firm to handle the sale while we managed the units.

For some reason, this new agent was condescending, rude, and just not likable. He did, however, speak the same language as the property owner, so he was hired. During a meeting, he was being extremely difficult and arrogant, making everyone uncomfortable. He had the listing; he spoke two languages. He also wore skinny jeans and did not hold back when applying cologne. Luckily, we were still wearing COVID masks, but our eyes were burning. This guy was controlling the sale while being a total jerk. How could this happen?

One of our agents was perplexed at how a guy like this could get any business. A huge reason was that he spoke a second language and had a few years in the business. Even a blind squirrel gets a nut occasionally, as the saying goes. This guy was woefully unaware of how negatively he was perceived.

But the problem with being unlikeable is that you leave so much on the table. Whatever money he made, he could've tripled if he was kind, nice, respectful, and fun. He was so busy being an ass that he hurt his own business. *So stupid.* Some people don't know what they don't know.

Choose your persona wisely. Your happiness level depends on it. You don't have to bake chocolate chip cookies for every neighbor who contracts COVID-19, but a simple hello or short conversation will take you far when you need to borrow a pickup truck.

LIFE LESSON

Be aware of the persona you're projecting.

DON'T SUCK

DON'T
SUCK

...AT DEALING WITH COVID

ANDRE'S TEN-DAY COVID-19 FESTIVAL

"I have no clue how I got COVID. I am surprised."

—RANDHIR KAPOOR

On Saturday, December 12, 2020, I tested positive for COVID-19.

Andre LeClair

60 years old

205 pounds

Five foot eleven

Self-employed

Physically fit

Residing in Bedford, New Hampshire, and Sarasota, Florida

Since March 2020, I'd always worn a mask, maintained social distance, and washed my hands frequently. I worked in the real estate field but didn't take chances. I oversaw my business from a home office, rarely going out except to the food store or occasional restaurant.

I flew to Sarasota on business the second week of December. The plan was to return to New Hampshire for Christmas and then back to Sarasota for most of the winter.

By mid-week, I felt quite sick and drove to a state-sponsored testing site. Fifteen minutes after my test, a text confirmed I was positive for COVID-19. And it was *on!*

I went back to my condo for a Zoom call with the doctor. He explained that treatments, administered via IV, required in-patient hospital admission. He prescribed cough medicine, steroids, and an antibiotic. He told me to rest and drink fluids. He suggested a pulse oximeter to measure my blood oxygen levels.

My sense of taste and smell were gone, as was my appetite. I felt exhausted and sick, and for the next few days, I was isolated in my condo, just riding it out. Because I was alone, I didn't realize I was not doing very well. I was drinking only a small amount of water and hadn't eaten any food for days.

I was hallucinating and saying crazy things. By day five, I was giving my cars away to a friend in New Hampshire. Unless you are Oprah or Elvis, giving away cars is a sign you might be hallucinating.

In 2001, my dad and I traveled together to Sarasota. I was on a mission to buy a vacation condo, and Dad was thrilled to accompany me. We had a blast, looking at properties by day and eating every night at his favorite Italian restaurant. We stayed in nice hotels and even had some beach time. It was a great father-son trip.

I settled on a condo, and sixty days later, he and I returned to get it furnished and ready. For many years, he often stayed at the condo and enjoyed all Sarasota had to offer. In 2014 at age eighty-three, Dad passed away, but I have always felt his presence at the condo. Being isolated with COVID made the feelings that much stronger.

The day before I was taken to the hospital, I sat on the lanai, wanting to call him. I also vaguely remember having a conversation with him on my cell. I cried like a baby, asking him to come down from heaven to be with me (and the group of soldiers I was forming to protect the clubhouse and pool area). I even offered to pay for takeout from The Italian Grille. I guess Papa was busy and couldn't make it, but it was comforting to chat with him.

I was hallucinating, had no food for six days, and was in rough shape. My friends called an ambulance. Hazmat-suited medics strongly suggested that instead of waiting for my soldiers, it may be best to head to the hospital. I could barely walk.

After two attempts at jumping out of the ambulance, I reached the hospital. I was given a red mesh hat, which distinguished me as a COVID-positive patient, and taken to the COVID floor. Everyone was wearing hazmat suits, so it was like *Ghostbusters*. I got intravenous fluids and felt a bit better.

The next day, I was treated with antiviral medication and some donated antibodies. I was in the hospital for four days. All the while, I felt extremely sick, weak, and defeated. Where the hell were my soldiers?

SARASOTA MEMORIAL HOSPITAL

The hospital staffers were phenomenal, never complaining. They had to suit up every time they entered my room, and it just seemed so aggravating to me, but I heard not a single complaint...ever.

I engaged with everyone and thanked them for being so wonderful. A young guy showed up very late to take blood. I asked him how I could become handsome like he was. Without hesitation, he told me to work on my hair. The kid had it! I was told I was a favorite patient. I didn't want to be sick, and I felt bad they had to take care of me. All of them were spectacular.

After my hospital stay, I was dropped at home and told to isolate. I was coming back from the brink, but I was coughing and sweating...a lot. I was soaked from head to toe, as if someone had sprayed me with a garden hose. COVID is a bear. I was sweating, freezing, and feeling sick, hoping I wouldn't relapse because I just wanted it to be over.

This was also when I discovered grocery delivery. Eating a can of soup per day, I was down twenty pounds.

My friend called to say he sold the car and got a decent price for it. *What car?*

A nice lady from the condo complex called to find out if it was true that I had "the covids."

"Andre, is it true you have the covids?"

"Yes, ma'am. It's true."

"All nineteen of them?"

A TRILLION DOLLARS

If I ever obtain a degree in chemistry, I plan to assemble a team of scientists to isolate the part of the COVID virus that takes away appetite. Imagine not being hungry. For me, something about COVID eliminated my desire to eat. If I could separate out and bottle the appetite suppressant from the virus, I'd make a trillion dollars and no longer need to buy Powerball tickets. I'm quite confident about this, so eat all the donuts you like for now. I'll keep you posted.

In the end, I realized COVID-19 is just a part of life, and life isn't always picture-perfect, nor is it meant to be. As I said before, if every day were sunny, we would all burn to death. The suffering and loss of time I experienced made me a stronger and better man. I consider myself incredibly lucky to be alive, unscathed, and able to tell my story. I learned so much about myself and my world. It is unbelievable to me that so many amazing people work in healthcare. They deserve to be honored.

Thank you to all my sweet and caring friends who brought me stuff, checked in, and even called an ambulance (I still think I could have lived a few more days, but...). And thanks to my wonderful family members, my colleagues, and my mama, who racked up forty-four hours of cell usage checking on me. All that lovin' is worth more than a trillion dollars!

LIFE LESSON ————————————————————————————

Be the best you can be, and create a life you love.

———————————————————————————— DON'T SUCK

ACKNOWLEDGMENTS

I would like to thank everyone who encouraged me to write this book, and more importantly, I would like to extend my most sincere thanks to everyone who told me I could never do it!